hamlyn
QuickCook

hamlyn
QuickCook
Desserts

Recipes by Denise Smart

Every dish, three ways—you choose!
30 minutes | 20 minutes | 10 minutes

An Hachette UK Company
www.hachette.co.uk

First published in Great Britain in 2012 by Hamlyn,
a division of Octopus Publishing Group Ltd,
Endeavour House, 189 Shaftesbury Avenue,
London, WC2H 8JY, UK
www.octopusbooks.co.uk

Distributed in the US by Hachette Book Group USA
237 Park Avenue, New York, NY 10017 USA
www.octopusbooksusa.com

Distributed in Canada by Canadian Manda Group
165 Dufferin Street, Toronto, Ontario, Canada M6K 3H6

ISBN 978-0-600-62399-1

Printed and bound in China

10 9 8 7 6 5 4 3 2 1

Standard level spoon and cup measurements are used in all recipes, unless
otherwise indicated.

Ovens should be preheated to the specified temperature. If using a convection oven,
follow the manufacturer's instructions for adjusting the time and temperature.
Broilers should also be preheated.

This book includes dishes made with nuts and nut derivatives. It is advisable for
those with known allergic reactions to nuts and nut derivatives and those who may
be potentially vulnerable to these allergies, such as pregnant and nursing mothers,
people with certain chronic illnesses, the elderly, babies, and children, to avoid dishes
made with nuts and nut oils.

It is also prudent to check the labels of prepared ingredients for the possible inclusion
of nut derivatives.

The U.S. Department of Agriculture advises that eggs should not be consumed raw.
This book contains some dishes made with raw or lightly cooked eggs. It is prudent
for more vulnerable people, such as pregnant and nursing mothers, those with
weakened immune systems, the elderly, babies, and young children, to avoid dishes
made with raw or lightly cooked eggs.

Contents

Introduction

30, 20, 10—Quick, Quicker, Quickest

This book offers a new and flexible approach to meal-planning for busy cooks, letting you choose the recipe option that best fits the time you have available. Inside you will find 360 dishes that will inspire and motivate you to get cooking every day of the year. All the recipes take a maximum of 30 minutes to cook. Some take as little as 20 minutes and, amazingly, many take only 10 minutes. With a little preparation, you can easily try out one new recipe from this book each night and slowly you will be able to build a wide and exciting portfolio of recipes to suit your needs.

How Does it Work?

Every recipe in the QuickCook series can be cooked one of three ways—a 30-minute version, a 20-minute version, or a super-quick-and-easy 10-minute version. At the beginning of each chapter, you'll find recipes listed by time. Choose a dish based on how much time you have and turn to that page.

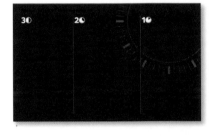

You'll find the main recipe in the middle of the page accompanied by a beautiful photograph, as well as two time-variation recipes below.

If you enjoy your chosen dish, why not go back and cook the other time-variation options at a later date? So, if you liked the 20-minute Mango and Passion Fruit Tart, but only have 10 minutes to spare this time around, you'll find a way to cook it using clever shortcuts.

If you love the ingredients and flavors of the 10-minute Strawberries with Meringue, why not try something more substantial, such as the 20-minute Meringues with Strawberry Cream, or be inspired to make a more elaborate version, such as the Baked Strawberry Meringue Pie? Or, browse through all 360 delicious recipes, find something that catches your eye, then cook the version that fits your time frame.

Or, for easy inspiration, turn to the gallery on pages 12–19 to get an instant overview by themes, such as Crowd Pleasers or Deliciously Decadent.

QuickCook online

To make life even easier, you can use the special code on each recipe page to email yourself a recipe card for printing, or email a text-only shopping list to your phone. Go to www.hamlynquickcook.com and enter the recipe code at the bottom of each page.

UTI-KUI-JOL-KOL

QuickCook Desserts

The busy lives that we lead today tend to leave us little time to make a delicious dessert from scratch. However, whether you crave something fruity or chocolatey, or a dessert to tempt your family or entertain your friends, you will find something for every occasion in this book. There is also a chapter containing healthier options, so by reducing the fat and using healthier ingredients and cooking methods, you can still enjoy a delicious dessert.

The secret of the perfect dessert is to make sure you have chosen the right one as part of a meal. So if you have a heavy main dish, choose a light fruity dessert, or a pastry or chocolate dessert can follow a lighter main dish. The time of year will also influence your choice, so in winter you might be craving a warming comforting dessert, whereas in summer something fruitier and lighter will be appropriate. Make use of fruits when they are in season and plentiful, because they will taste so much better then, even when served simply with a scoop of ice cream or grilled with a sprinkling of sugar.

QuickCook Techniques and Tips

Anyone can make a fantastic dessert if they have the right cooking equipment on hand; a well-equipped kitchen will help you save time and get the best results.

A handheld electric mixer is a great time-saving device when it comes tomaking desserts, and makes beating up meringues or sponge cakes a speedy process.

A food processor is indispensable and can crush cookies, chop nuts, blend fruit purees and coulis and make bread crumbs, sponge cake mixes, cookies, and pastry in no time. The microwave can be used to melt chocolate and butter.

A set of standard measuring spoons and cups are essential for accurate measuring. Also, make sure that you have at least two sharp knives—a small one for paring and slicing and a larger one for chopping—and remember that a sharpened knife is much safer than a blunt one. In addition, it's a good idea to invest in a selection of metal or plastic pastry cutters in different sizes, an apple corer, cherry pitter, grater or microplane for removing rind from citrus fruits, pastry brushes, and a rolling pin.

A selection of mixing bowls (make sure they are spotlessly clean) will be required for beating egg whites and cream, and for mixing batters and other mixtures.

Keep a good supply of nonstick baking sheets of different sizes, a jelly roll pan, and a supply of parchment paper, aluminum foil, and plastic. You will also need a nonstick skillet, along with a set of saucepans.

To save time, many of these desserts are made in smaller baking pans and dishes, so muffin and cupcake pans, individual tart pans, ramekins or custard cups, ovenproof dishes, and dariole or metal dessert molds will be needed. Use the right size pan and dish to make sure that your desserts are perfect.

QuickCook Ingredients

Make sure that your pantry is well stocked at all times; it's amazing how easy it is to create a quick dessert from the staple items in your kitchen pantry. Cans of fruit can be made into quick crisps or fruit fools and are a great substitute when certain fruits are out of season. Store-bought meringue nests and shells can be filled with cream and fruit, or crumbled up for a quick Strawberries with Meringues (see page 134). Crushed cookies make a great base for cheesecakes, can add texture to baked fruits, or can be soaked in alcohol and placed in the bottom of fools or zabagliones. Cans of condensed and evaporated milk make a great substitute for fresh milk and cream and a can of caramel can be used to make a speedy Banana Caramel Pie (see page 130).

Always make sure that you have a supply of all-purpose and self-rising flours, cocoa powder, and baking powder in the pantry. A selection of sugars, such as superfine, granulated, and light brown, are essential, and it's a good idea to keep some honey on hand, along with light corn syrup and maple syrup. Eggs are another staple ingredient; unless stated otherwise, all eggs used in the recipes in this book are large.

Chocolate also appears frequently in the recipes in this book—particularly in the Heavenly Chocolate chapter. When buying dark chocolate, choose one with over 70 percent cocoa solids to help the desserts set more quickly.

Store-bought cakes make a simple base for trifles as well as substitutes for ladyfingers; alternately, make simple sponge-based desserts, from sliced banana, chocolate, and ginger cake, baked for a short time with your favorite sauces.

Store-bought chocolate or caramel sauces, fruit compotes, and fruit sauces make great toppings for ice cream and sundaes, fillings for pancakes, or bases for brûlées. Ground spices, such as ginger, nutmeg, and cinnamon, can add a delicious twist, too.

Experiment with different breads, such as fruit bread, panettone, and brioche, for quick bread and butter puddings, cinnamon toas,t or for the base of a tart.

Finally, store-bought large or small piecrusts can be quickly filled and transformed into luscious lemon-flavored or fruit-filled tarts.

The Refrigerator and Freezer

Make sure you use your freezer. Frozen bags of tropical fruits or mixed berries can be made into crisps, ice cream, or sorbets. A short time in the freezer will help set gelatins and mousses within their alloted time limit.

Toda,y there is no need to waste precious time making your own pastry; flaky, puff, and phyllo pastries can be bought chilled and frozen and transformed into fantastic desserts, such as apple or apricot tarts, millefeuilles, and strudels.

Always keep in the freezer a good-quality vanilla ice cream and a fruit sorbet, so you can whip up a dessert in no time.

When making toppings for crips, make double and freeze one portion; that way you will always have the bare bones of a dessert on hand. When fruits are in season, stew them, then store in the freezer. These can be used for crisps or fools.

Keep your refrigerator filled with a fresh supply of butter, milk, plain yogurt, heavy cream or crème fraîche, whipped cream, and cream cheese or mascarpone cheese so that you will always be able to create a tasty treat. Many of these ingredients can also be used as accompaniments to serve with desserts.

Flavorings

Flavors can be easily imparted into your desserts. Buy fruit syrups, such as black currant syrup or elderflower syrup (look for an online supplier) to add flavoring to cream or fruit syrups. For something a little more luxurious, a splash of rum or brandy, or a liqueur, such as one flavored with orange, black currant, or almond, can be added to your dessert to enhance the flavor. You can also buy cinnamon, lavender, or vanilla sugars—or why not make your own vanilla sugar by placing superfine sugar in a jar along with a split vanilla bean from which you have used the seeds to make a dessert?

Add a citrus kick to your dessert by beating the grated rinds of lemons, limes, and oranges in butter and sugar. Use chocolate that has been infused with ginger, orange, mint, or chili flavorings to make a speedy chocolate sauce. Buy natural vanilla, almond, and lemon extracts because they have better flavors than imitation ones. More unusual flavors can be obtained from Asian ingredients, such as lemongrass, fresh ginger, green tea, and spices, such as cardamom, cinnamon, and star anise. Fresh herbs, such as rosemary, basil, and lemon thyme, can also be used to impart aromatic flavors.

Presentation

They say the first bite is with the eye, so the way you present your desserts is of the highest importance. It takes just a few creative finishing touches to make your dessert look really luscious and professional. These can be incredibly simple, such as a dusting of confectioners' sugar or unsweetened cocoa powder, a scattering of fresh fruit or grated chocolate, or a drizzle of melted chocolate. Store-bought cookies, such as Florentines, almond thins, macaroons, biscotti, and amaretti are the perfect accompaniment to a dessert. If you have a little more time, scoop ice cream into tuile baskets (see page 236) or serve it with Salted Caramel Shards (see page 192). Or create impressive chocolate curls by spreading melted dark, white, or milk chocolate about ¼ inch thick on a marble slab, letting it stand to just set, then drawing a wallpaper scraper or knife held at a 45-degree angle across the chocolate.

Especially for summer

Delicious desserts that capture the flavors of summer.

Thai Fruit Skewers 30

Apricot and Marzipan Pastries 42

Baked Peaches with Raspberries and Amaretti 64

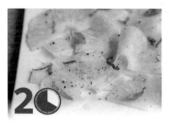

White Chocolate, Lemongrass, and Cardamom Mousse 104

Raspberry Millefeuille 200

Meringues with Rosewater and Pomegranate 218

Carpaccio of Pineapple with Basil 242

Grillled Mango with Lime and Chile Syrup 252

Mango, Cardamom, and Mint Fools 256

Watermelon with Mint Sugar 268

Tropical Fruit Salad with Ginger Green Tea Syrup 276

Gooseberry and Elderflower Fools 278

Winter comfort

Tasty desserts to warm you up on a cold winter day.

Spiced Oven-roasted Plums 34

Baked Apricots and Blueberries 50

Plum Oatmeal Crisp 52

Rhubarb and Ginger Tarte Tatins 68

Chocolate Risotto 96

Bananas and Pecans with Butterscotch Custard 138

Date, Maple Syrup, and Pecan Puddings 148

Mincemeat and Apple Strudel 170

Quick Rosewater and Cardamom Rice Pudding 174

Banana and Caramel Tarte Tatin 202

Spiced Dried Fruit Compote 248

Blackberry and Apple Puffs 258

Berry nice

Liven up your desserts with all things berry.

Raspberry and Honey Cranachan 26

Blueberry and Vanilla Trifles 48

Passion Fruit and Strawberry Phyllo Tarts 62

Blackberry Charlotte 70

Blueberry Baskets with White Chocolate Sauce 88

Blueberry Pancakes 132

Strawberries with Meringues 134

Blueberry and Lemon Sponge Puddings 160

White Chocolate and Raspberry Meringue Roulade 190

Easy Blackberry Fool 238

Floating Islands with Elderflower Syrup and Berries 266

Baked Red Fruit and Hazelnut Meringues 270

Chilled out

Frozen and chilled desserts, and ideas for toppings.

Tropical Fruit and Basil Ice Cream 24

Chocolate Fudge Sauce 78

Chocolate and Cherry Ice Cream Sundaes 80

Chocolate Sorbet Bites 106

Rocky Road Ice Cream Sundaes 144

Chocolate and Apricot Crunch 166

Affogato al Caffe 184

Salted Caramel Shards 192

Mini Baked Alaskas 212

Coconut and Lime Gelatins 214

Frozen Berry Yogurt Ice Cream 236

Instant Raspberry Sorbet 274

Kids' favorites

Make these desserts to give your kids a treat.

Poached Rhubarb on Fruit Bread 44

Pineapple Upside-Down Puddings 60

Free-Form Nectarine and Almond Pie 66

Pear and Chocolate Crisps 98

Chocolate Pancakes 102

Spiced Chocolate Sponge with Belgian Chocolate Sauce 112

Fruity Chocolate Bread and Butter Pudding 120

Warm Marshmallow Dip with Fruit Kabobs 142

Sesame Banana Fritters with Peanut Butter Sauce 146

Creamy Lemon and Almond Rice Pudding 154

Vanilla Poached Pears with Warm Fudge Sauce 198

Banana and Buttermilk Pancakes 260

Mini mouthfuls

Individual servings of some of your favorite desserts.

Phyllo Apple Pies 54

Individual Black Currant Cheesecakes 72

Chocolate-Dipped Fruit 82

Sour Cherry Chocolate Brownie Puddings 90

Chocolate Blinis 92

Mini Molasses Tarts 158

Baked New York Cheesecakes 164

Brandy Snaps with Limoncello Cream 204

Portuguese Custard Tarts 210

Lavender Crème Brûlées 222

Hot Mango and Passion Fruit Soufflés 224

Mini Baked Cappuccino Cheesecakes 226

Crowd pleasers

Tarts, pies, and other desserts to please your family and friends.

Mango and Passion Fruit Tart 38

White Chocolate and Strawberry Cheesecake 108

Chocolate and Cherry Trifle 110

Chocolate and Ginger Tart 114

Apricot, Chocolate, and Brioche Tart 118

Gooey Chocolate and Prune Torte 122

Banana-Caramel Pie 130

Sherry Trifle 150

Key Lime Pie 152

Apple Tart 162

Tangy Lemon Tarts 188

Orange and Rosemary Polenta Cake 216

Deliciously decadent

Luscious desserts for that special treat.

Cherry Clafoutis 46

Chocolate Espresso Pots 86

Chocolate and Pistachio Soufflés 116

Chocolate Mousse with Honeycomb 124

Chocolate Fondue with Hazelnut Straws 176

Tiramisu 182

Irish Coffee Syllabubs 194

Pan-Fried Figs with Marsala 196

Banana and Irish Cream Trifles 206

Chocolate Cups with Mint Syllabub 208

Chocolate Zabaglione 228

Parmesan and Rosemary Thins with Poached Grapes 230

QuickCook
Fruity
Treats

Recipes listed by cooking time

3

2

 # Tropical Fruit and Basil Ice Cream

Serves 4–6

14½ oz frozen tropical fruits, such as mango, papaya, and pineapple

1 tablespoon lime juice

scant 1 cup mascarpone cheese

2 tablespoons confectioners' sugar

2 tablespoons chopped basil, plus 4–6 basil sprigs, to decorate

- Place half the fruit and the lime juice in a food processor and process until coarsely chopped. Add the mascarpone and confectioners' sugar and blend until fairly smooth.

- Add the remaining fruit and the basil and blend in short bursts until no large lumps of fruit remain. Scoop into bowls and serve immediately, decorated with basil sprigs.

2 Tropical Ice Cream Coconut Sandwiches

Make the ice cream as above and add 1 large spoonful onto one side of 1 coconut chocolate macaroon or cookie and top with another cookie. Place in the freezer. Repeat with another 10 cookies. Remove the ice cream sandwiches from the freezer and serve, 2 per person, immediately.

3 Individual Tropical Ice Cream Bombes

Make the ice cream as above and spoon into six ⅔ cup metal molds or ramekins, cover with plastic wrap, and freeze for 20 minutes. To serve, dip the bottoms of the dishes briefly in hot water and invert onto serving plates. Serve drizzled with store-bought mango coulis.

 # Raspberry and Honey Cranachan

Serves 4

½ cup rolled oats
2 tablespoons whiskey
1 cup heavy cream
2 cups raspberries
3 tablespoons honey

- Place the oats in a nonstick skillet over medium heat and dry-fry for 2–3 minutes, stirring continuously, until toasted. Transfer to a plate to cool.

- Meanwhile, whip the whiskey and cream with a handheld electric mixer in a bowl until it forms soft peaks. Place a handful of the raspberries in a separate bowl and crush with a fork.

- Stir the oats, honey, crushed raspberries, and remaining raspberries into the whiskey cream. Spoon into 4 glasses and serve immediately.

2 Oat, Raspberry, and Honey Sundaes

Mix together 2 tablespoons whiskey, 1 tablespoon honey, and the grated rind and juice of ½ lemon in a small bowl. Place 1¼ cups heavy cream in a large bowl and pour in the honey mixture, then beat with a handheld electric mixer until the cream starts to thicken. Divide ½ cup honey granola among 4 glasses, then spoon heaping ½ cup raspberries over the granola. Spoon half the cream into the glasses. Repeat the layers, finishing with the cream. Chill for 5–10 minutes before serving.

3 Oat and Raspberry Cranachan Trifle

Slice 2 shortcakes in half and arrange in the bottom of a 6 inch bowl. Pour over 2 tablespoons whiskey, then scatter over 1½ cups raspberries. Top with 1 cup granola and drizzle with 2 tablespoons honey. Mix together 1 cup prepared vanilla pudding or custard (see page 150) and 1 tablespoon whiskey, to taste, and pour over the granola. Lightly whip 1 cup heavy cream in a bowl with a handheld electric mixer until it forms soft peaks, then spoon on top of the trifle. Decorate with extra raspberries, cover, and chill for 15 minutes before serving.

 # Fast Fruit Brûlée

Serves 4

11½ oz store-bought fruit
  compote, such as mixed berries
2 cups Greek yogurt
⅓ cup Demerara sugar

- Spoon the fruit compote into four ⅔ cup ramekins. Spoon the yogurt over the compote, then sprinkle over the sugar. Place on a baking sheet.

- Cook under a preheated hot broiler for 4–5 minutes or until the sugar is brown and bubbling. Let cool for 3–4 minutes before serving.

2 Tipsy Caramelized Mixed Berries

Place 3 cups frozen mixed berries in a shallow ovenproof dish. Pour over 2 tablespoons black currant syrup, then sprinkle over 2–3 tablespoons Demerara sugar. Cook under a preheated hot broiler for 10–15 minutes or until the sugar has caramelized. Serve with vanilla ice cream or over the Vanilla Cream Custard Pots.

3  Vanilla Cream Custard Pots with Fruit Compote

Chill four ⅔ cup ramekins while you make the filling. Place 3 egg yolks, 1 tablespoon instant vanilla pudding mix, 3 tablespoons vanilla sugar, and 3 tablespoons milk in a heatproof bowl and beat together. Warm 1 cup milk in a saucepan, then gradually beat into the egg mixture. Return to the pan and cook over medium heat, whisking continuously, for 3–4 minutes, until the custard has thickened. Let cool slightly, then beat in ¾ cup mascarpone cheese until smooth, and finally beat in an additional ¾ cup mascarpone. Pour the mixture into the ramekins and chill for 15 minutes. Serve topped with 11½ oz store-bought fruit compote.

Thai Fruit Kebabs

Serves 4

4 long lemon grass stalks

2 kiwifruit, peeled, each cut into 8 pieces

2 mangoes, peeled, pitted, and cut into ¾ inch pieces

1 papaya, peeled, seeds removed, and cut into ¾ inch pieces

½ pineapple, skinned, cored, and cut into ¾ inch pieces (see page 242)

2 tablespoons light brown sugar

2 tablespoons dried coconut

vanilla yogurt, to serve (optional)

- Cut the lemon grass stalks into 8 inch lengths and cut each in half lengthwise. Remove the tough outer layers and trim one end of each stalk to make a point (this makes skewering the fruit easier).

- Thread the fruit alternately onto 8 lemon grass skewers, then place in a single layer on a baking sheet. Mix together the sugar and coconut in a small bowl, then sprinkle over the fruit.

- Cook under a preheated hot broiler for 1–2 minutes or until the sugar caramelizes and the coconut is toasted. Serve immediately, accompanied by vanilla yogurt, if using.

---

2 **Thai Fruit Kebabs with Coconut Custard** Prepare the fruit skewers as above. Place 1 cup coconut milk, 1 cup milk, 2 egg yolks, 2 tablespoons superfine sugar, and 1 teaspoon cornstarch in a small saucepan. Beat, without boiling, over low heat for 5–10 minutes until the custard has thickened. Broil the fruit kebabs as above and serve with the warm custard.

3 **Thai Fruit Salad in Lemon Grass Syrup** Remove the tough outer layers of 2 lemon grass stalks and bash with a rolling pin to break the stalks open and release the flavor. Place in a saucepan with ¾ cup superfine sugar and 1 cup water and stir over low heat until the sugar has dissolved. When it starts to boil, take the pan off the heat and pour into a heatproof pitcher. Chill for 20 minutes, letting the lemon grass infuse, until the syrup is cold. Meanwhile, prepare the fruit as above and gently mix together in a large bowl. Strain over the syrup and stir in the juice of 2 limes. Serve immediately.

2  Melon and Blueberry Salad with Thyme Syrup

Serves 6

½ cup superfine sugar
1 cup cold water
3 lemon thyme sprigs, plus extra
  to decorate
2 strips of lemon peel
½ honeydew melon
½ cantaloupe melon
½ small watermelon
1 cup blueberries

- Place the sugar, measured water, lemon thyme, and lemon peel in a saucepan over medium heat. Bring to a boil, then reduce the heat and simmer for 5 minutes until reduced by half.

- Let cool for 5 minutes, then pour into a pitcher and chill for an additional 10 minutes. Strain the syrup to remove the lemon peel and thyme.

- Meanwhile, remove the skin and seeds from the melons and cut the flesh into cubes. Place in a bowl with the blueberries, then pour over the cooled syrup and stir well.

- Spoon into bowls with some of the syrup and serve decorated with a few sprigs of lemon thyme.

---

1 Melon and Mint Salad

Prepare the melons as above and place in a bowl. Stir in 2 tablespoons chopped mint and the grated rind and juice of 1 lime. Sprinkle with a little sea salt and serve immediately.

3 Melon, Ginger, and Cilantro Salad

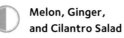

Place ½ cup superfine sugar, a 1 inch piece of peeled fresh ginger root, cut into thin strips, and 1 cup water in a saucepan and bring to a boil, stirring until the sugar has dissolved. Reduce the heat and simmer for 5 minutes. Pour into a heatproof pitcher and chill for 20 minutes. Meanwhile, remove the skin and seeds from ½ cantaloupe melon, ½ galia melon, and ½ honeydew melon and cut into thin slices. Place in a bowl and strain over the cooled syrup, then scatter with 3 tablespoons chopped fresh cilantro.

 Spiced Oven-Roasted Plums

Serves 4

8 ripe red plums
1 cinnamon stick
2 star anise
¼ cup Demerara sugar
grated rind and juice of 1 orange
2 tablespoons orange liqueur
2 tablespoons water

- Place the whole plums, cinnamon stick, and star anise in a shallow ovenproof dish. Scatter over the sugar, then add the orange rind and juice, orange liqueur and measured water.

- Place in a preheated oven, at 400°F, for 25–30 minutes, basting halfway through the cooking time.

- Spoon the plums into bowls and pour over some of the syrup. Serve immediately.

1 **Spiced Plum Compote**

Place 1 lb halved and pitted plums in a saucepan with 1 cup orange juice, 2 tablespoons light brown sugar, 1 cinnamon stick, and 2 star anise. Cook, uncovered, over low heat for 10 minutes or until the plums are tender. Remove the cinnamon stick and star anise and serve with vanilla yogurt.

2 **Vanilla Oven-Roasted Plums**

Place 8 halved and pitted plums in an ovenproof dish. Dot with 2 tablespoons unsalted butter and sprinkle over 2 tablespoons vanilla sugar. Place in a preheated oven, at 400°F, for 10–15 minutes or until softened and caramelized. Serve with vanilla yogurt.

Caramelized Oranges with Cinnamon Tortillas

Serves 4

4 large oranges

6 tablespoons unsalted butter, slightly softened

¼ cup superfine sugar

2 tablespoons confectioners' sugar

1 teaspoon ground cinnamon

4 soft flour tortillas

- Finely grate the rind of 2 of the oranges. Using a sharp knife, cut the tops and bottoms from all the oranges and remove the skin and pith. Hold the oranges over a bowl to collect the juice and cut out the segments.

- Melt 4 tablespoons of the butter in a skillet, add the superfine sugar, scant ½ cup of the reserved orange juice, and half the rind, and cook over medium heat, stirring occasionally, until the sugar has dissolved. Simmer for 4–5 minutes until thickened and syrupy. Stir in the orange segments to heat through.

- Meanwhile, mix the remaining butter and orange rind with the confectioners' sugar and cinnamon. Arrange the tortillas on a large baking sheet, then brush one side with the butter mixture. Place in a preheated oven, at 400°F, for 2–3 minutes or until golden. Let cool slightly, then cut each into 4 triangles. Spoon the oranges and syrup into bowls and serve with the tortilla triangles.

 Cinnamon Crepes with Chocolate Orange Sauce Make 8 crepes (see right), adding 1 teaspoon cinnamon to the batter, and keep warm. Melt 3 oz orange-flavored dark chocolate, broken into small pieces, with ⅔ cup heavy cream in a heatproof bowl set over a saucepan of gently simmering water. Cut the tops and bottoms from 3 large oranges, then remove the skin and pith and cut into segments. Fold the crepes into quarters and fill with the orange segments. Serve drizzled with the chocolate sauce.

 Orangey Crêpes Suzette Sift ¾ cup all-purpose flour and a pinch of salt into a large bowl and make a well in the center. Pour in 2 beaten eggs, then gradually beat into the flour. Gradually add 1¼ cups milk, beating to form a smooth batter. Stir in 2 tablespoons melted, unsalted butter. Heat a little more butter in an 8 inch nonstick crepe pan or skillet. Add a ladleful of batter to coat the bottom of the pan. Cook for 1–2 minutes until golden, then flip and cook for 1 minute. Repeat with the remaining batter to make 8 pancakes and keep warm. To make the syrup, put 7 tablespoons softened unsalted butter and ½ cup superfine sugar in a bowl and beat with a handheld electric mixer until creamy, then beat in the grated rind and juice of 1 orange and 2 tablespoons orange liqueur. Place the mixture in a large skillet and boil rapidly for 2 minutes. Reduce the heat and add the crepes one at a time, folding each one in half and then into quarters in the syrup, until hot. Warm 2 tablespoons orange liqueur and 1 tablespoon brandy in a small saucepan, set alight, and pour over the crepes.

DES-FRUI-XUZ

Mango and Passion Fruit Tart

Serves 6–8

1 cup mascarpone cheese

3 tablespoons confectioners' sugar, sifted

2 tablespoons lime juice

scant ½ cup canned mango puree

8 inch store-bought piecrust

1 ripe mango, peeled, pitted, and sliced

2 passion fruit

- Place the mascarpone in a bowl and beat with a wooden spoon until softened. Stir in the confectioners' sugar, lime juice, and mango puree until well combined. Spoon into the piecrust and spread the top level. Chill for 15 minutes.

- Arrange the sliced mango over the top of the tart, cut the passion fruit in half, and while holding over the tart scoop out the seeds and juice and drizzle over the mango. Serve immediately.

---

1 — Mango and Passion Fruit Yogurt Crunch

Mix together 2 cups Greek yogurt, ⅓ cup confectioners' sugar, sifted, and 1 tablespoon lime juice in a bowl. Peel, pit, and chop 2 mangoes into small cubes and divide amoung six 1 cup glasses. Spoon half the yogurt mixture over the top and spoon over the seeds and juice from 2 passion fruit. Divide ½ cup granola among the glasses and finish with the remaining yogurt and the seeds and juice from 1 passion fruit.

3 — Mango and Passion Fruit Tarte Tatin

Place ¼ cup superfine sugar, 2 tablespoons unsalted butter, and the pulp of 2 passion fruit in a 9 inch skillet with an ovenproof handle and cook over low heat, stirring, until the butter has melted and the sugar has dissolved. Simmer for 2–3 minutes until the mixture is syrupy. Arrange 2 peeled, pitted, and sliced mangoes over the syrup. Unroll a 12 oz package chilled puff pastry and cut out a circle slightly larger than the skillet. Place the circle of pastry over the skillet, tucking the edges loosely around the edges so that steam can escape. Place in a preheated oven, at 400°F, for 20–25 minutes or until the pastry is puffed and golden. Let stand in the skillet for a few minutes to cool slightly. Using an oven mitt, place a serving dish on top of the skillet and turn upside down. Scrape any remaining sauce over the tarte tatin.

 # Coconut Creams with Mango

Serves 4

⅔ cup half-and-half
¼ teaspoon coconut extract
1 cup Greek yogurt
½ cup confectioners' sugar, sifted
2 tablespoons dried coconut
1 ripe mango, peeled, pitted,
   and chopped

- Pour the half-and-half and coconut extract into a bowl, then beat in the yogurt and confectioners' sugar. Spoon into 4 small glasses, then chill until ready to serve.

- Meanwhile, place the dried coconut in a small skillet and dry-fry over medium heat, stirring, until lightly toasted. Let cool.

- Spoon the mango over the top of the coconut creams. Sprinkle over the toasted coconut and serve.

2 Grilled Mango with Coconut

Using a sharp knife, remove the skin from 2 mangoes, then cut each one into thick slices from both sides of the pit. Place the mango in a preheated ridged grill pan and cook for 5 minutes on each side. Transfer to 4 serving plates and squeeze over the juice of 2 limes. Slice the flesh of ½ coconut into thin slithers, then place in the griddle pan and cook for 1 minute on each side until toasted. Serve sprinkled over the mango.

3 Coconut Rice Pudding with

Mango Place ½ cup rinsed short-grain rice, 3 tablespoons superfine sugar, and 2 cups boiling water in a saucepan and bring to a boil. Reduce the heat and simmer, uncovered, for 10 minutes. Pour in 1¾ cups coconut milk and simmer for an additional 15–20 minutes, stirring occasionally, until the rice is tender. Serve with chopped mango and toasted coconut.

Apricot and Marzipan Pastries

Serves 6

12 oz package chilled rolled
   puff pastry
6 oz marzipan, coarsely chopped
3 tablespoons heavy cream,
   plus extra to serve (optional)
9 apricots, halved and pitted
¼ cup slivered almonds

- Unroll the pastry and cut into six 6½ x 3½ inch rectangles, then place on a baking sheet. Using a sharp knife, score a ½ inch border around the edge, but do not cut all the way through. Prick the center of each rectangle with a fork. Chill while you make the filling.

- Place the marzipan and cream in a food processor or blender and blend until smooth.

- Spoon a blob of the marzipan mixture onto each pastry rectangle and spread it up to the border. Arrange 3 apricot halves on top of the marzipan, cut side up, and sprinkle over the almonds.

- Place in a preheated oven, at 400°F, for 12–13 minutes or until risen and golden. Serve warm with heavy cream, if using.

1   Grilled Apricots with Marzipan

Halve and pit 12 apricots and arrange the halves, cut side up, in a shallow ovenproof dish. Divide 5 oz marzipan into 24 pieces and roll into small nuggets, then place in the centers of the apricots. Sprinkle with 3 tablespoons light brown sugar and ¼ cup slivered almonds. Cook under a preheated hot broiler for 5–6 minutes until the sugar starts to caramelize.

3   Apricot and Almond Tart

Unroll a 12 oz package chilled rolled puff pastry onto a large baking sheet, then sprinkle over ½ cup ground almonds. Arrange about 1¾ lb halved and pitted apricots over the top, right up to the edge of the pastry. Sprinkle over 2 tablespoons light brown sugar. Place in a preheated oven, at 400°F, for 20–25 minutes or until risen and golden.

 # Poached Rhubarb on Fruit Bread

Serves 4

1 tablespoon unsalted butter

¼ cup packed light brown sugar

1 teaspoon peeled and grated
   fresh ginger root

grated rind and juice of ½ orange

12 oz rhubarb, trimmed and cut
   into 5 inch lengths

4 slices fruit bread or panettone,
   1 inch thick

vanilla ice cream, to serve

- Place the butter, sugar, ginger, and orange rind and juice in a skillet large enough to hold the rhubarb in a single layer and cook over low heat until the sugar has dissolved. Add the rhubarb and simmer gently for 5 minutes, then turn over and cook for an additional 2–3 minutes until tender.

- Meanwhile, lightly toast the bread. Arrange 3–4 strips of rhubarb on top of each, then drizzle over the syrup. Serve immediately with scoops of vanilla ice cream.

2 Quick Rhubarb Trifles

Place 1 lb rhubarb, trimmed and chopped, ¼ cup superfine sugar, and 1 teaspoon vanilla extract in a saucepan. Cover and simmer for 5–7 minutes until tender, then let cool slightly. Place 4 slices of fruit bread or panettone, cut to fit, in the bottom of 4 glasses, then spoon the rhubarb and any syrup over the top. Spoon 4 cups prepared vanilla pudding or custard (see page 150) over the rhubarb. Lightly whip 1¼ cups heavy cream in a bowl with a handheld electric mixer until it forms soft peaks, then spoon on top of the trifles. Chill until ready to serve.

3 Individual Rhubarb and Vanilla Pies

Place 1 lb rhubarb, trimmed and cut into 1 inch pieces, in a bowl and stir in ⅓ cup superfine sugar, 1 piece of preserved ginger in syrup, finely chopped, and the grated rind of 1 orange. Spoon the rhubarb mixture and the juice into four deep, 1 cup ovenproof dishes and spoon 1 cup prepared vanilla pudding or custard (see page 150) over the tops. Unroll a 12 oz package chilled rolled puff pastry and cut out 4 circles slightly larger than the dishes. Place a pastry top over the pies and brush the tops with a little beaten egg. Make a hole in the middle for the steam to escape. Place on a baking sheet and bake in a preheated oven, at 375°F, for 20–25 minutes or until golden and bubbling. Let stand for 5 minutes before serving.

 Cherry Clafoutis

Serves 4

butter, for greasing

32 fresh or canned cherries, pitted

4 tablespoons kirsch

3 tablespoons superfine sugar

3 tablespoons all-purpose flour, sifted

4 eggs, beaten

½ cup heavy cream

6 tablespoons milk

½ teaspoon vanilla extract

confectioners' sugar, for dusting (optional)

- Grease four 1 cup ramekins or ovenproof dishes and place on a baking sheet. Divide the cherries evenly among the dishes and spoon 1 tablespoon of the kirsch over each.

- Place the sugar, flour, and eggs in a bowl and beat together with a handheld electric mixer until light and well blended. Whisk in the cream, milk, and vanilla extract.

- Pour the batter over the top of the cherries and place the dishes in a preheated oven, at 375°F, for 20–25 minutes or until the batter has set. Serve immediately, dusted with confectioners' sugar, if using.

1 **Cherry Jubilee**
Drain a 14 oz can pitted cherries in juice, reserving the juice. Mix 1 tablespoon of the cherry juice with 1 tablespoon superfine sugar and 2 teaspoons cornstarch in a small bowl. Place the remaining cherry juice with the cornstarch mixture in a skillet and whisk until thickened, then add the cherries and warm through. Pour in 3 tablespoons warmed kirsch, then set alight to burn off the alcohol. Scoop 2 large scoops of vanilla ice cream into each of 4 glasses, then pour the cherries over the top. Serve immediately.

2 **Mini Cherry and Almond Clafoutis**
Grease 8 cups of a 12-cup nonstick muffin pan and put 4 pitted cherries in the bottom of each. Place 2 tablespoons superfine sugar, 2 tablespoons all-purpose flour, 2 eggs, and 1 teaspoon almond extract in a bowl and beat together with a handheld electric mixer until blended. Whisk in 6 tablespoons heavy cream. Spoon the batter into the muffin pan cups and sprinkle over 2 tablespoons slivered almonds. Place in a preheated oven, at 400°F, for 12–15 minutes until risen and golden. Serve 2 clafoutis per person with a spoonful of heavy cream.

Blueberry and Vanilla Trifles

Serves 6

2 cups blueberries,
  plus extra to decorate
¼ cup superfine sugar
2 tablespoons black currant syrup
1 tablespoon water
8 oz store-bought pound cake,
  cubed
2 cups prepared vanilla pudding
  or custard (see page 150)
1¼ cups heavy cream
¼ cup slivered almonds, toasted

- Place the blueberries, sugar, black currant syrup, and measured water in a small saucepan and cook over low heat, stirring, until the sugar has dissolved. Cook gently for 2–3 minutes until the berries start to burst, then pour into a bowl and chill for 10 minutes.

- Divide the cake between 6 glasses and spoon over the blueberries and their juice. Spoon the custard over the tops.

- Lightly whip the cream with a handheld electric mixer in a bowl until it forms soft peaks, then spoon over custard. Decorate with the extra blueberries and toasted almonds. Serve immediately or chill until ready to serve.

---

10 Waffles with Blueberry and Lemon Sauce Place 2 cups blueberries, the grated rind and juice of 1 lemon, and ¼ cup superfine sugar in a saucepan and cook over low heat, stirring, until the sugar has dissolved. Cook gently for 2–3 minutes until the berries start to burst. Meanwhile, lightly toast 6 waffles and place in bowls. Add a scoop of vanilla ice cream to each, then pour over the warm sauce and serve immediately.

---

30 Balsamic Blueberry Trifle Place 2 cups blueberries, 2 tablespoons superfine sugar, 2 teaspoons balsamic vinegar, and 1 tablespoon water in a saucepan and cook gently for 3–4 minutes until the berries start to burst, then pour into a bowl and chill for 10 minutes. Coarsely chop 2 blueberry muffins and arrange in the bottom of a large bowl, then spoon over the blueberries and let soak. Meanwhile, blend together ¼ cup superfine sugar, 2 teaspoons instant vanilla pudding mix, 2 teaspoons cornstarch, and 1 tablespoon milk in a heatproof bowl to form a paste, then beat in 1 egg yolk.

Put 1½ cups milk and 1 teaspoon vanilla extract in a saucepan and heat until just below boiling point. Stir into the cornstarch paste, then pour into a clean saucepan. Cook over medium heat, whisking continuously, until the pudding has thickened. Remove from the heat and stir in 1 cup reduced-fat crème fraîche until smooth. Pour into a bowl, cover with plastic wrap to prevent a skin from forming, and chill. Spoon the chilled custard over the blueberries. Lightly whip 1¾ cups heavy cream in a bowl with a handheld electric mixer until it forms soft peaks, then spoon on top of the trifle. Serve immediately or chill until ready to serve.

Baked Apricot and Blueberries

Serves 4

12 ripe apricots, halved
  and pitted
1 cup blueberries
2 tablespoons light brown sugar
1⅓ cups self-rising flour,
  plus extra for dusting
4 tablespoons unsalted butter,
  diced
¼ cup superfine sugar
½ cup buttermilk
milk, for brushing

- Place the apricots and blueberries in a 1-quart ovenproof dish and sprinkle over the brown sugar.

- Place the flour in a bowl, add the butter, and rub in with the fingertips until the mixture resembles fine bread crumbs. Stir in the superfine sugar, then add the buttermilk, a little at a time, to form a slightly sticky, soft dough.

- Turn the dough out onto a lightly floured surface and pat out until it is ½ inch thick. Cut out 8 circles using a 2½ inch cutter.

- Arrange over the top of the fruit and brush with a little milk. Place in a preheated oven, at 350°F, for 20 minutes or until the topping is golden and the fruit is bubbling. Serve immediately.

1 Apricot and Blueberry Compote

Place 8 halved and pitted apricots, 1 cup blueberries, 2 tablespoons light brown sugar, and 1 tablespoon water in a saucepan and cook over low heat for 5–7 minutes, stirring occasionally, until the blueberries start to burst and the apricots have softened. Serve with dollops of Greek yogurt and drizzled with honey.

2 Apricot and Blueberry with Crumb Topping

Mix together 1 cup blueberries and 2 drained, 14 oz cans apricot halves in juice in a bowl and sprinkle over 2 tablespoons light brown sugar. Spoon into 4 ovenproof dishes. Mix 10 tablespoons melted, unsalted butter with ⅔ cup light corn syrup and 1 cup rolled oats, then scatter over the fruit. Place on a baking sheet and bake in a preheated oven, at 375°F, for 15 minutes or until golden.

 Plums with Oat Topping

Serves 6

9–10 ripe plums, (about 2 lb), halved and pitted
1 teaspoon vanilla extract
2 tablespoons light brown sugar
whipped cream, to serve (optional)

For the topping

10 tablespoons unsalted butter
⅔ cup light corn syrup
½ teaspoon salt
2 cups rolled oats
¼ cup slivered almonds

- To make the topping, gently melt the butter, corn syrup, and salt in a saucepan. Remove from the heat and stir in the oats and almonds.

- Meanwhile, cut the plums into quarters, or smaller if large. Place in an ovenproof dish and sprinkle over the vanilla extract and sugar.

- Pile the topping over the plums, allowing some of the fruit to poke through. Place in a preheated oven, at 375°F, for 25 minutes or until the topping is golden and the plums have softened. Serve with whipped cream, if using.

1 Plum, Yogurt, and Granola Layer

Pit and quarter 12 plums and divide among 6 glasses. Divide 2½ cups granola among the glasses and spoon ¼ cup vanilla yogurt over each. Serve immediately.

2 Individual Red Plums with Crumb Topping

Divide two 20 oz cans plums in syrup among 6 shallow ovenproof dishes, halving the plums if necessary, and spoon ¼ cup of the syrup over each. Make the topping as above, then pile over the plums. Place on a baking sheet and bake in a preheated oven, at 375°F, for 10–12 minutes or until golden and bubbling.

Phyllo Apple Pies

Serves 6–8

3 Granny Smith apples (about
  1 lb 5 oz), peeled, cored, and
  cut into ½ inch pieces
½ cup packed light brown sugar
grated rind and juice of ½ lemon
½ teaspoon ground cinnamon
⅓ cup golden raisins
7 oz phyllo pastry
4 tablespoons unsalted butter,
  melted
confectioners' sugar, for dusting
vanilla ice cream or light cream,
  to serve (optional)

- Place the apples, sugar, lemon rind and juice, cinnamon, and raisins in a large saucepan and cook gently for 5 minutes, stirring occasionally, until the apples have softened but still hold their shape. Let cool slightly.

- Meanwhile, cut the pastry into thirty-two 5½ inch squares, reserving the trimmings. Cover the pastry with a damp cloth to prevent it from drying out. Take one of the squares and brush with butter, then place another square over the top at an angle to make a star shape. Repeat with 2 more squares of pastry, brushing each with butter. Gently press into a cup of a 12-cup nonstick muffin pan. Repeat with the remaining pastry to make 8 pastry shells.

- Fill each shell with the apple mixture, then brush the trimmings with butter, scrunch up, and place on top of the pies. Place in a preheated oven, at 375°F, for 15 minutes or until golden brown. Serve 1–2 pies per person, dusted with confectioners' sugar and accompanied by scoops of vanilla ice cream or light cream, if using.

 Apple and Blackberry Compote Melt 4 tablespoons unsalted butter in a large saucepan. Stir in ¼ cup superfine sugar, then add 3 peeled, cored, and chopped dessert apples and 2 tablespoons apple jack or apple juice. Cook for 4–5 minutes, stirring, until the apples are golden brown and tender. Stir in 1½ cups blackberries and cook for an additional 3–4 minutes until they start to release their juice. Serve with vanilla ice cream.

 Baked Apple Rings Keeping the apples whole, peel and core 6 small Granny Smith apples, then cut each into 4 thick rings. Place in a buttered roasting pan. Mix together ½ teaspoon ground cinnamon, ½ teaspoon ground ginger, 3 tablespoons honey, and 1 cup raisins in a bowl and spoon the mixture into the center of the apples. Add ¼ cup water and place in a preheated oven, at 400°F, for 15 minutes.

30 Rhubarb, Orange, and Almond Crisps

Serves 4

13 oz rhubarb, trimmed and
  cut into 1 inch pieces
⅓ cup superfine sugar
juice of 1 small orange

For the topping

1 cup all-purpose flour
6 tablespoons unsalted
  butter, diced
¼ cup superfine sugar
¼ cup ground almonds
grated rind of 1 small orange

- Place the rhubarb, sugar, and orange juice in a large bowl and stir well.

- To make the topping, place the flour in a bowl, add the butter, and rub in with the fingertips until the mixture resembles fine bread crumbs. Alternatively, use a food processor. Stir in the sugar, almonds, and orange rind.

- Spoon the rhubarb mixture and juice into four 1 cup ovenproof dishes. Sprinkle over the topping and press down lightly.

- Place on a baking sheet and bake in a preheated oven, at 375°F, for 20–25 minutes or until golden and bubbling.

1 **Speedy Rhubarb and Orange Compote** Place 13 oz rhubarb, prepared as above, the grated rind and juice of 1 small orange, and 2 tablespoons superfine sugar in a saucepan. Cover with a lid and simmer for 5–7 minutes until tender. Serve warm, spooned over vanilla ice cream.

2 **Rhubarb and Orange Fools** Place 13 oz rhubarb, prepared as above, with ⅓ cup superfine sugar, the grated rind of ½ orange, and 1 tablespoon orange juice in a saucepan and simmer for 8–10 minutes until tender. Let cool slightly, then place in a food processor or blender with ¾ cup prepared vanilla pudding or custard (see page 150) and blend until well combined. Spoon into 4 glasses and chill until ready to serve. Serve topped with a handful of toasted, slivered almonds.

 # Orange and Cranberry Puddings

Serves 4

7 tablespoons unsalted
    butter, softened, plus
    extra for greasing
grated rind of ½ small orange
7 tablespoons superfine sugar
1 tablespoon light corn syrup
2 eggs
1 cup self-rising flour, sifted
½ cup dried cranberries
whipped cream, to serve

For the sauce

3 tablespoons chunky orange
    marmalade
1 tablespoon cranberry jelly
2 tablespoons orange juice

- To make the sauce, place all the ingredients in a saucepan and heat gently until the marmalade and cranberry jelly are dissolved. Bring to a boil, then reduce the heat and simmer gently for 5 minutes to form a thick syrup.

- Meanwhile, grease four 1 cup ramekins or metal molds and line the bottom with nonstick parchment paper. Place on a baking sheet and spoon the sauce into the bottom of each.

- Place the butter, orange rind, sugar, and corn syrup in a large bowl and beat together with a handheld electric mixer until light and fluffy. Beat in the eggs, one at a time, then gently fold in the flour and cranberries.

- Spoon the pudding mixture into the dishes and place in a preheated oven, at 375°F, for 20 minutes or until risen and set.

- Turn out the puddings onto serving plates and serve with dollops of whipped cream.

---

1 **Orange and Cranberry Puree**

Place ⅔ cup superfine sugar and ⅔ cup fresh orange juice in a saucepan and stir over low heat until the sugar has dissolved. Add 1¾ cups cranberries and cook over low heat for 7–8 minutes until the cranberries have popped. Place in a food processor or blender and blend to form a puree, then press through a strainer into a bowl. Delicious stirred into yogurt.

2 **Individual Orange and Cranberry Upside-Down Cakes**

Melt 1 tablespoon butter in a skillet and add 2 tablespoons superfine sugar. Stir in ⅔ cup cranberries and cook for 2–3 minutes until syrupy. Spoon the mixture into 4 greased cups of a 6-cup nonstick muffin pan. Meanwhile, place ⅔ cup self-rising flour, ⅓ cup superfine sugar, 6 tablespoons softened unsalted butter, the grated rind of 1 orange, and 1 egg in a food processor or blender and blend until combined. Spoon the mixture over the berries. Place in a preheated oven, at 350°F, for 12–15 minutes until risen and golden. Turn out the cakes onto serving plates and serve warm.

 # Pineapple Upside-Down Puddings

Serves 4

2 tablespoons unsalted butter

¼ cup packed light brown sugar

4 canned pineapple rings in juice, drained

4 candied cherries

For the sponge

7 tablespoons unsalted butter, softened, plus extra for greasing

½ cup superfine sugar

2 eggs

1⅓ cups self-rising flour

¼ teaspoon ground allspice

- Lightly grease four 1 cup ramekins or metal molds and place on a baking sheet.

- Melt the butter in a small saucepan, add the sugar, and cook until the sugar has dissolved. Pour into the prepared dishes, then place a pineapple ring in each dish and a cherry in the center of each ring.

- To make the sponge, place the butter and sugar in a large bowl and beat together with a handheld electric mixer until light and fluffy, then beat in the eggs. Gently fold in the flour and allspice.

- Spoon the batter into the dishes and spread the tops level. Place in a preheated oven, at 350°F, for 20 minutes or until risen and firm to the touch. Let cool in the ramekins for a few minutes.

- Turn out the puddings onto plates and serve immediately.

---

1 Broiled Cinnamon Pineapple Rings

Cut the top and bottom off 1 pineapple. Hold the pineapple firmly, resting it on the cut bottom. Slice off the skin, working from top to bottom, removing any brown "eyes." Cut into ½ inch thick circles and remove the tough core using an apple corer. Mix together 3 tablespoons light brown sugar and 1 teaspoon ground cinnamon on a plate. Dip the pineapple rings in 4 tablespoons melted unsalted butter, then coat in the cinnamon sugar mixture. Place on a baking sheet and cook under a preheated hot broiler for 3–4 minutes or until caramelized.

2 Pineapple in Warm Spiced Syrup

Place ½ cup superfine sugar, 1 inch piece of peeled fresh ginger root, cut into thin strips, 1 cinnamon stick, and 1 cup water in a small saucepan and bring to a gentle simmer, stirring until the sugar has dissolved. Remove from the heat and stir in the juice of 1 lemon. Slice the skin from the pineapple (see left). Cut into quarters lengthwise, remove the tough core, and cut into thick slices. Place in a heatproof bowl and pour over the warm syrup. Let stand for 15 minutes to cool slightly.

Passion Fruit and Strawberry Phyllo Tarts

Serves 6

7 oz phyllo pastry
1 tablespoon sunflower oil
scant 1 cup mascarpone cheese
1 tablespoon confectioners'
  sugar, plus extra for dusting
  (optional)
2 passion fruit
⅔ cup hulled and sliced
  strawberries

- Cut the pastry into twenty-four 5 inch squares. Cover the pastry with a damp cloth to prevent it from drying out. Take one of the squares of pastry and brush with a little oil. Place another square over the top at an angle to make a star shape. Repeat with 2 more squares of pastry, brushing each with oil. Gently press into a hole of a 6-cup nonstick muffin pan. Repeat with the remaining pastry to make 6 pastry shells.

- Place in a preheated oven, at 350°F, for 5 minutes or until golden. Remove the shells from the pan and cool on a wire rack.

- Meanwhile, place the mascarpone and confectioners' sugar in a bowl and beat together. Cut the passion fruit in half and scoop the juice and seeds into the mixture. Stir well, then spoon into the cooled shells.

- Decorate with the strawberries and dust with confectioners' sugar, if using. Serve immediately.

---

10 Warm Passion Fruit Curd Tarts

Place ½ cup passion fruit pulp (about 5 passion fruit) and 7 tablespoons unsalted butter in a saucepan over low heat and stir until the butter has melted. Whisk in ⅓ cup superfine sugar, 1 whole egg, and 3 egg yolks, then cook over low heat, whisking continuously, for 5–6 minutes until the mixture has thickened. Fill six 3½ inch store-bought pastry shells with the passion fruit curd and serve warm with hulled and sliced strawberries.

30 Shortcake with Passion Fruit and Mascarpone Cream

Place 2 cups self-rising flour in a bowl, add 4 tablespoons diced unsalted butter, and rub in with the fingertips until the mixture resembles fine bread crumbs. Stir in ¼ cup superfine sugar and ½–⅔ cup milk and mix to form a soft dough. Turn out onto a lightly floured surface and knead briefly until smooth. Roll out and gently press into a greased 8 inch, loose-bottom, round cake pan. Place in a preheated oven, at 400°F, for 15–20 minutes or until risen, firm to the touch, and golden brown. Let cool in the pan for 5 minutes, then turn out onto a wire rack and cool completely. Meanwhile, make the mascarpone-and-passion fruit mixture as above and serve with the shortcake, decorated with hulled and sliced strawberries.

Baked Peaches with Raspberries and Amaretti

Serves 4

4 ripe peaches, halved and pitted
1 cup raspberries
1 cup mascarpone cheese
1 tablespoon almond liqueur
6 amaretti cookies, crushed
2 tablespoons honey

- Place the peach halves in a shallow ovenproof dish, cut side up. Spoon the raspberries into the centers and over the top.

- Mix together the mascarpone, almond liqueur, and crushed cookies in a bowl, then spoon over the peaches. Drizzle with the honey.

- Place in a preheated oven, at 400°F, for 10 minutes or until the mascarpone has melted.

- Spoon the peaches into bowls, spooning over the sauce and raspberries, and serve immediately.

Simple Peach Melba

Drain 8 canned peach halves and place 2 halves in each of 4 glasses. Place 2 cups raspberries, ⅓ cup confectioners' sugar, and 2 teaspoons lemon juice in a food processor or blender and blend to form a puree, then press through a strainer into a bowl to remove the seeds. Add a scoop of vanilla ice cream to each of the glasses and drizzle with the raspberry sauce. Serve immediately.

Peach and Raspberry Pudding

Halve, pit, and slice 2 peaches and arrange in the bottom of a shallow ovenproof dish. Add 1 cup raspberries and crumble over 6 amaretti cookies. Mix together 1 cup mascarpone cheese, 1 tablespoon almond liqueur, and 2 tablespoons superfine sugar in a bowl. Spoon over the fruit and sprinkle the top with 2 tablespoons Demerara sugar. Place in a preheated oven, at 350°F, for 20 minutes.

30 Free-Form Nectarine and Almond Pie

Serves 4–6

1 lb chilled puff pastry
flour, for dusting
¼ cup ground almonds
6 ripe nectarines, halved,
  pitted, and quartered
1 beaten egg
2 tablespoons Demerara sugar
2 tablespoons slivered almonds
confectioners' sugar, for dusting
heavy cream, to serve (optional)

- Roll out the pastry on a lightly floured surface to about a 12 inch circle and place onto a large baking sheet. Sprinkle over the ground almonds, then pile the nectarines in the center of the pastry.

- Brush the edges of the pastry with a little of the beaten egg, then bring the pastry edges into the center, leaving the fruit exposed in the middle. Scrunch up the edges of the pastry, then brush with more beaten egg. Sprinkle over the sugar and slivered almonds.

- Place in a preheated oven, at 400°F, for 20–25 minutes or until the pastry is browned.

- Dust the warm pie with confectioners' sugar and serve in slices with heavy cream, if using.

---

1 **Hazelnut Cream Shortbreads with Nectarines** Lightly whip ⅔ cup heavy cream in a bowl with a handheld electric mixer until it forms soft peaks. Stir in ¼ cup chopped, toasted hazelnuts, then spoon on top of 8–12 shortbread cookies. Halve and pit 2 nectarines and cut into slices. Arrange over the cream and serve immediately.

2 **Baked Nectarines with Pistachios and Almonds** Halve and pit 4 ripe nectarines and place in a buttered ovenproof dish, cut side up. Place ½ cup shelled pistachio nuts, 3 macaroons, and 2 tablespoons light brown sugar in a food processor and process to form fine bread crumbs. Add 4 tablespoons softened unsalted butter and 2 oz marzipan and process to form a paste. Spoon a tablespoon of the mixture into each nectarine cavity and drizzle 2 tablespoons almond liqueur over the top. Scatter with 2 tablespoons slivered almonds and place in a preheated oven, at 400°F, for 15 minutes or until softened and golden.

 # Rhubarb and Ginger Tarte Tatins

Serves 4

4 rhubarb stalks, trimmed
and cut into 1 inch pieces

2 tablespoons unsalted butter

2 pieces of preserved ginger
in syrup, finely chopped

¼ cup preserved ginger syrup
(taken from the jar)

12 oz package chilled rolled
puff pastry

vanilla ice cream or light cream,
to serve (optional)

- Divide the rhubarb among four 4 inch metal pie plates or tart pans. Place the butter, chopped preserved ginger, and ginger syrup in a small saucepan and bring to a boil. Pour the ginger mixture evenly over the rhubarb.

- Unroll the pastry and cut out circles, using a cutter slightly larger than the dishes. Place the pastry circles over the dishes, tucking the edges loosely around the edges so that steam can escape.

- Place in a preheated oven, at 400°F, for 10–12 minutes or until the pastry is puffed and golden. Let stand in the dishes for a few minutes to cool slightly.

- Using an oven mitt, place a serving plate on top of each dish and turn upside down. Scrape any remaining sauce in the dishes over the tarte tatins. Serve immediately with vanilla ice cream or light cream, if using.

Rhubarb and Ginger Compote

Place 1 lb rhubarb, prepared as above, in a saucepan with 2 pieces of preserved ginger in syrup, chopped, 2 tablespoons preserved ginger syrup, and 1 tablespoon superfine sugar. Cover with a lid and cook over low heat for 7–10 minutes, stirring occasionally, until tender. Serve warm with dollops of Greek yogurt.

Individual Rhubarb and Ginger Crisps

Place 1½ lb rhubarb, prepared as above, in a bowl with 2 pieces of preserved ginger in syrup, finely chopped, 2 tablespoons preserved ginger syrup, and 2 tablespoons superfine sugar. Mix together and spoon into four 1 cup ovenproof dishes. Place 1⅓ cups all-purpose flour and ½ cup rolled oats in a bowl, add 7 tablespoons diced unsalted butter, and rub in with the fingertips until the mixture resembles fine bread crumbs. Alternatively, use a food processor. Stir in ¼ cup superfine sugar and sprinkle over the rhubarb. Place on a baking sheet and bake in a preheated oven, at 350° F, for 20–25 minutes or until bubbling.

DES-FRUI-BEH

Blackberry Charlotte

Serves 4

3½ cups blackberries
¾ cup superfine sugar
1 teaspoon vanilla extract
8 small, thin slices of white bread
2 tablespoons unsalted butter,
  softened
whipped cream, to serve
  (optional)

- Place the blackberries in an ovenproof dish, then gently stir in the sugar and vanilla extract.

- Cut the crusts from the bread, spread both sides with the butter, and cut in half to form triangles. Arrange over the blackberries, overlapping slightly in 2 rows.

- Place in a preheated oven, at 375°F, for 20–25 minutes or until the bread is golden and crisp and the fruit bubbling. Serve with whipped cream, if using.

1 Blackberry Compote

Place 3 cups blackberries, ⅔ cup superfine sugar, and 3 tablespoons black currant syrup in a saucepan and cook over low heat, stirring, until the sugar has dissolved. Simmer for 4–5 minutes until the blackberries have softened and started to release their juice. Serve spooned over vanilla ice cream.

2 Individual Blackberry Charlotte Puddings

Place 2¾ cups blackberries and ¾ cup superfine sugar in a saucepan and cook for 2–3 minutes or until the blackberries have started to break down. Cut the crusts from 12 slices of white bread, then, using a cutter, stamp out 4 circles to fit the mold bottoms and 4 larger circles for the tops. Cut the remaining bread into strips.

Dip each piece of bread in 8 tablespoons (1 stick) melted unsalted butter and use to line the bottom and sides of the molds. Spoon the blackberries and any juice into 4 greased dariole molds, then top with the larger circles of bread. Place on a baking sheet and bake in a preheated oven, at 400°F, for 8–10 minutes or until golden. Let cool in the molds for a few minutes. Turn out the puddings into bowls and serve cream.

 Individual Black Currant Cheesecakes

Serves 6

1 cup crushed Graham crackers

4 tablespoons unsalted butter, melted

1 envelope gelatin

½ cup boiling water

½ cup evaporated milk, chilled

½ cup cream cheese

½ cup black currants, blueberries, or other berries of your choice

a few fresh black currants, blueberries, or other berries, to decorate

- Stir the crushed cookies into the melted butter and press into the bottom of six 3½ inch, loose-bottom, round tart pans. Chill while you make the filling.

- Place the gelatin in a heatproof pitcher and pour over the measured water. Stir until it is fully dissolved.

- Whisk the evaporated milk in a large bowl with a handheld electric mixer until light and fluffy and doubled in volume. Whisk in the cream cheese until there are no lumps and the mixture is smooth, then whisk in the gelatin. Stir in the fruit and mix well.

- Pour over the cookie bases and let chill for 15 minutes or until set. Serve decorated with extra fruit.

1 Black Currant Coulis

Place 2 cups black currants or berries and ⅓ cup superfine sugar in a food processor or blender and blend until smooth, then press through a strainer into a bowl. Serve the coulis poured over ice cream.

2 Black Currant Milk Gelatins

Place an envelope of gelatin in a heatproof pitcher and pour over ½ cup boiling water. Stir until it is fully dissolved. Whisk a chilled 13 oz can evaporated milk in a large bowl with a handheld electric mixer until doubled in volume, then whisk in the gelatin. Stir in 1 cup frozen black currants or other berries, until they start to release their juice, then pour into 6 glasses. Chill for 10 minutes until set.

QuickCook

Heavenly Chocolate

Recipes listed by cooking time

3⟳

2⟳

Chocolate Fudge Sauce

Serves 6

1 cup heavy cream
¾ cup packed light brown sugar
2 tablespoons unsalted butter
¼ cup light corn syrup
½ cup milk
7 oz semisweet dark chocolate
(72 percent cocoa solids),
broken into small pieces
ice cream, to serve

- Place the cream, sugar, butter, light corn syrup, and milk in a heavy saucepan and heat gently until the sugar has dissolved and the butter has melted. Bring to a boil, then boil for 5 minutes, stirring continuously, until thick and smooth.

- Remove from the heat, add the chocolate, and stir until melted. Let cool slightly, then pour over ice cream.

2 Knickerbocker Glories with Chocolate Fudge Sauce

Make the sauce as above. Chop 3 double chocolate muffins and divide half among 6 tall sundae glasses. Add 1 large scoop of strawberry ice cream to each glass and top with 3 hulled and halved strawberries. Drizzle 2 tablespoons of the warm sauce over each sundae, then repeat the layers, finishing with the sauce. Serve each sundae decorated with a strawberry.

3 Simple Gooey Chocolate Fudge Pudding Make the sauce as above. Meanwhile, slice a 11½ oz store-bought chocolate cake into ½ inch thick slices and arrange in the bottom of a 1-quart ovenproof dish. Spoon over 1 cup of the sauce. Place in a preheated oven, at 350°F, for 20 minutes or until bubbling.

Chocolate and Cherry Ice Cream Sundaes

Serves 4

3 cups cherries, halved and pitted
¼ cup kirsch or cherry syrup
16-oz container vanilla ice cream
2 double chocolate muffins,
   coarsely chopped
½ cup store-bought
   chocolate sauce
1¼ cups heavy whipping cream

To serve

4 cherries on their stems
a little grated chocolate

- Place a few of the cherries in the bottom of 4 tall sundae glasses and spoon 1 tablespoon of the kirsch or cherry syrup into each glass. Add 2 small scoops of vanilla ice cream to each glass. Divide half the muffin pieces among the glasses and spoon 1 tablespoon chocolate sauce over each.

- Repeat with another layer of cherries, ice cream, muffins, and chocolate sauce, finishing with an extra layer of cherries.

- Lightly whip the cream in a bowl with a handheld electric mixer until soft peaks form and spoon over the sundaes. Decorate with the cherries on their stems and a little grated chocolate. Serve immediately with long spoons.

---

2 **Cherry and Chocolate Brownie Squares** Cut 4 store-bought chocolate brownies in half crosswise to make thin slices. Lightly whip 1¼ cups heavy cream with a handheld electric mixer in a bowl until it forms soft peaks, then spread half the whipped cream over 4 of the brownie squares. Top each one with 3 cherries taken from a jar of cherries in kirsch, then top with the remaining brownie slices. Press down lightly, then spoon the remaining cream on top and top with 3 more cherries and a drizzle of the kirsch. Chill for 10 minutes before serving to let the flavors mingle.

3 **Tipsy Cherry and Chocolate Puddings** Divide 2½ cups pitted cherries among 4 small glasses. Place 4 extra-large egg yolks, ¼ cup unsweetened cocoa powder, and ⅓ cup superfine sugar in a large heatproof bowl and beat with a handheld electric mixer until thick and creamy. Set the bowl over a saucepan of simmering water and gradually beat in ½ cup Marsala. Continue beating for another 10 minutes or until the mixture thickens. Remove from the heat and beat for a few more minutes. Pour over the cherries and serve immediately.

Chocolate-Dipped Fruit

Serves 6

4 oz white chocolate,
broken into small pieces
4 oz semisweet dark chocolate,
broken into small pieces
1 lb strawberries, with stems
1 cup red cherries, with stems
1 cup Cape gooseberries, yellow
cherries, with stems, or other
fruit of choice, prepared,
if necessary

- Melt the chocolate in 2 separate heatproof bowls set over saucepans of gently simmering water, then let cool slightly.

- Line a baking sheet with nonstick parchment paper. Dip a selection of the fruit halfway into the dark chocolate and let the excess drip back into the bowl. Place on the baking sheet to set. Dip the remaining fruit halfway into the white chocolate and place on the baking sheet. Chill for 10–15 minutes until set.

1 — White Chocolate Dipping Sauce with Fruit

Place 8 oz coarsely chopped white chocolate, ⅔ cup heavy cream, 4 tablespoons diced unsalted butter, and 1 teaspoon vanilla extract in a small heatproof bowl set over a saucepan of simmering water. Heat gently for 5–7 minutes, stirring occasionally, until smooth and glossy. Pour into a warm bowl and serve immediately with 1 lb strawberries, with stems, 1 cup cherries, with stems, and 1 large, sliced banana for dipping.

3 — Chocolate Fruit Bowl

Melt 8 oz semisweet dark chocolate, broken into small pieces, in a heatproof bowl set over a saucepan of gently simmering water. Meanwhile, lay two 12 inch square pieces of aluminum foil together and fold the edges over to secure, then place over an upturned 2½ cup ovenproof bowl. Mold the foil around the bowl, smoothing out to remove the creases. Carefully remove the foil from the bowl and turn the right way up and flatten out the bottom. Using a spoon, spread the chocolate over the inside of the foil, leaving a ragged edge at the top. Place in the freezer for 10 minutes to firm up, then chill in the refrigerator for 10 minutes until set. Just before serving, quickly and carefully remove the foil and fill with 1 lb strawberries, with stems, 1 cup red cherries, with stems, and 1 cup Cape gooseberries, yellow cherries, with stems, or other fruit of choice.

Chocolate and Mandarin Cheesecakes

Serves 4

10-oz can mandarins
in juice
1 tablespoon superfine sugar
3 oz milk chocolate,
broken into small pieces
4 Graham crackers, crushed
⅔ cup cream cheese
½ cup heavy cream

- Drain the mandarins, reserving ½ cup of the juice. Place the reserved juice and sugar in a small saucepan and simmer for 3–4 minutes. Let cool.

- Meanwhile, melt the chocolate in a heatproof bowl set over a saucepan of gently simmering water, then let cool. Divide the crushed crackers amoung four small glasses.

- Place the cream cheese and heavy cream in a bowl and whisk together until just combined, then stir in the chocolate. Spoon into the glasses.

- Top with the mandarin slices, then drizzle over the cooled syrup. Serve immediately.

20 Mandarin and Chocolate Fools

Melt 4 oz semisweet or orange-flavored dark chocolate, broken into small pieces, in a heatproof bowl set over a saucepan of gently simmering water, then let cool. Put 1¼ cups store-bought vanilla pudding (or custard, see page 150) in a bowl and stir in the melted chocolate. Drain a 10-oz can of mandarins and divide among 4 glasses. Top with the pudding and chill for 10 minutes. Serve sprinkled with chocolate curls.

30 Upside-Down Mandarin and Chocolate Cake

Drain two 10-oz cans mandarins in juice. Arrange the mandarins over the bottom of an 20 cm (8 inch) loose-bottomed round cake pan lined with nonstick parchment paper. Place 2 eggs and ⅓ cup superfine sugar in a large bowl and beat with a handheld electric mixer until pale and thick and the beaters leave a trail when lifted above the mixture. Sift in ⅓ cup plus 1 tablespoon self-rising flour and ¼ cup unsweetened cocoa powder and gently fold in. Pour over the mandarins and place in a preheated oven, at 350°F, for 20–25 minutes or until firm to the touch. Let cool in the pan for a few minutes, then invert onto a plate and serve in slices.

 Chocolate Espresso Pots

Serves 4

4 oz semisweet dark chocolate (75–80 percent cocoa solids), broken into small pieces
2 teaspoons espresso powder
⅔ cup heavy cream
¾ cup Greek yogurt
4 chocolate-coated coffee beans, to decorate

- Chill four ½ cup espresso cups or ramekins while you make the filling.

- Melt together the chocolate, espresso powder, and 3 tablespoons of the cream in a heatproof bowl set over a saucepan of gently simmering water. Remove from the heat and stir in the remaining cream and half the yogurt.

- Pour into the chilled espresso cups or ramekins. Spoon the remaining yogurt over the top and decorate with a coffee bean. Chill for 10 minutes before serving.

---

1 Chocolate and Coffee Sauce

Melt 7 oz semisweet dark chocolate (75–80 percent cocoa solids), broken into small pieces, in a heatproof bowl set over a saucepan of gently simmering water. Stir in ½ cup hot strong black coffee, ½ cup heavy whipping cream, ¼ cup superfine sugar, and 1 tablespoon unsalted butter. Serve immediately poured over ice cream, chocolate brownies, or fruit.

3 Chocolate and Espresso Slices

Thinly roll out a 12 oz package chilled flaky pastry and use to line a 12 x 8 inch baking pan. Prick the bottom with a fork, then line with nonstick parchment paper and fill with pie weights or dried beans. Place in a preheated oven, at 400°F, for 10 minutes, then remove the paper and weights and return to the oven for an additional 2–3 minutes. Reduce the heat to 350°F. Meanwhile, melt 7 oz semisweet dark chocolate (75–80 percent cocoa solids), broken into small pieces, and 3 teaspoons espresso powder in a heatproof bowl set over a saucepan of gently simmering water. Place 2 extra-large eggs and ¼ cup packed light brown sugar in a bowl and beat with a handheld electric mixer until pale and fluffy, then beat in the melted chocolate mixture and ½ cup heavy cream. Fold in 3 tablespoons self-rising flour and pour into the pastry shell. Return to the oven and cook for 10 minutes. Let cool slightly, then dust with unsweetened cocoa powder and serve warm, cut into 8 slices, with dollops of crème fraîche.

Blueberry Baskets with White Chocolate Sauce

Serves 4

7 oz white chocolate
 (30 percent cocoa solids),
 broken into small pieces
4 brandy snap baskets
½ cup crème fraîche
1 piece of preserved ginger in
 syrup, finely chopped
1 tablespoon preserved ginger
 syrup (taken from the jar)
3 cups frozen blueberries

· Melt 2 oz of the white chocolate in a heatproof bowl set over a saucepan of gently simmering water. Spoon a little into each brandy snap basket, covering the bottom and sides (this will prevent the sauce from running out). Chill for 5 minutes.

· Meanwhile, melt the remaining chocolate, crème fraîche, preserved ginger, and preserved ginger syrup in a saucepan over low heat, stirring occasionally, until the ingredients have combined.

· Place the baskets on a plate and fill with the blueberries. Pour over the sauce and serve immediately.

2 **White Chocolate and Blueberry Baskets** Melt together 4 oz white chocolate (30 percent cocoa solids), broken into small pieces, and ½ cup heavy cream in a heatproof bowl set over a saucepan of gently simmering water. Let cool slightly, then stir in ½ cup crème fraîche. Spoon the mixture into 4 brandy snap baskets. Chill for 10 minutes, then top with ⅔ cup blueberries or raspberries.

3 **Blueberry and White Chocolate Pudding** Melt 4 oz white chocolate (30 percent cocoa solids), broken into small pieces, in a heatproof bowl set over a saucepan of gently simmering water. Place 4 tablespoons softened unsalted butter and ¼ cup superfine sugar in a large bowl and beat with a handheld electric mixer until light and fluffy. Whisk in 1 extra-large egg, ½ teaspoon vanilla extract, and the melted chocolate. Fold in 1 oz white chocolate chunks, ⅔ cup self-rising flour and ½ cup blueberries. Spoon into a 7 inch round cake pan lined with nonstick parchment paper and place in a preheated oven, at 350°F, for 20 minutes. Serve cut into wedges.

Sour Cherry Chocolate Brownie Puddings

Serves 4

6 tablespoons unsalted
  butter, softened, plus
  extra for greasing
½ cup packed light brown sugar
1 teaspoon vanilla extract
¼ cup unsweetened cocoa
  powder, sifted
⅓ cup plus 1 tablespoon
  self-rising flour, sifted
1 egg
⅓ cup dried sour cherries
heavy cream or crème fraîche,
  to serve

- Lightly grease 4 cups of a 6-cup nonstick muffin pan. Place the butter, sugar, and vanilla extract in a bowl and beat with a handheld electric mixer until light and fluffy.

- Add the cocoa powder, flour, and egg and beat until combined, then stir in the sour cherries.

- Spoon the mixture into the prepared muffin pan and place in a preheated oven, at 350°F, for 10–12 minutes or until just cooked but still soft in the centers.

- Turn out the puddings onto serving plates and serve immediately with heavy cream or crème fraîche.

Chocolate Brownie, Sour Cherry, and Ice Cream Sandwiches

Cut 4 store-bought chocolate brownies in half horizontally. Place a scoop of vanilla ice cream in the center of 1 half, then place another brownie half on top, pressing down gently. Place in the freezer. Repeat to make 4 ice cream sandwiches. Meanwhile, coarsely chop ½ cup dried sour cherries and place in a saucepan with 1 cup store-bought chocolate sauce. Warm through and pour over the brownies.

Chocolate and Sour Cherry Florentines

Melt 5 tablespoons unsalted butter in a saucepan, add ¼ cup superfine sugar, and heat gently until the sugar has dissolved. Bring to a boil, then remove from the heat and stir in 2 tablespoons heavy cream, 2 tablespoons chopped candied peel, ⅓ cup dried sour cherries, ½ cup slivered almonds, ⅓ cup chopped crystallized ginger, and 1 tablespoon all-purpose flour. Place heaping teaspoons of the mixture onto 2 greased nonstick baking sheets, spacing them well apart, and bake one sheet at a time in a preheated oven, at 350°F, for 8–10 minutes or until golden brown. Let cool on the baking sheets for 2 minutes, then transfer to a wire rack. Dip the edges of the cookies in 4 oz melted semisweet dark chocolate. Chill in the refrigerator for 10 minutes until set. Serve with chocolate ice cream.

Chocolate Blinis

Serves 6

¾ cup plus 1 tablespoon
self-rising flour

3 tablespoons unsweetened
cocoa powder

½ teaspoon baking powder

1 tablespoon superfine sugar

1 egg, beaten

¾ cup milk

1 tablespoon sunflower oil,
for frying

2 oz milk chocolate,
finely chopped

To serve

½ cup crème fraîche

1 cup raspberries

- Sift the flour, cocoa powder, and baking powder into a large bowl and stir in the sugar. Make a well in the center and gradually beat in the egg and a little of the milk to form a thick batter. Stir in the remaining milk.

- Heat a large nonstick skillet over medium heat. Using a scrunched up paper towel, dip into the oil and use to wipe over the skillet. Drop tablespoons of the batter into the skillet, spacing them well apart.

- Cook for 1 minute, then scatter a little of the chopped chocolate over each. Cook for an additional 1–2 minutes until bubbles start to appear on the surface and pop, then flip over and cook for an additional 1–2 minutes until just firm. Remove from the skillet and keep warm.

- Repeat with the remaining batter to make about 28 blinis, adding more oil if necessary. Serve warm, topped with crème fraîche and raspberries.

Quick Blinis with Chocolate Sauce

Warm through 24 store-bought blinis according to the package directions. Divide them among 6 serving dishes, then top each serving with ½ cup raspberries. Gently warm through 1 cup re-bought chocolate sauce in epan, pour over the blinis, e 4 blinis per person.

Chocolate Blinis with White Chocolate Ganache

To make the ganache, melt 5 oz white chocolate, broken into small pieces, in a heatproof bowl set over a saucepan of gently simmering water. Remove from the heat and stir in 1¼ cups crème fraiche and 1 tablespoon white crème de cacao, then chill until slightly thickened.

Meanwhile, make the blinis as above and let cool. Place a spoonful of the chilled ganache onto each blini and top with a raspberry. Dust with a little unsweetened cocoa powder and serve immediately.

Chocolate Orange Molten Lava Cakes

Serves 6

6 tablespoons unsalted
butter, softened, plus
extra for greasing
10 oz semisweet dark
chocolate (70 percent
cocoa solids), chopped
grated rind of 1 orange
⅓ cup packed light brown sugar
5 eggs
⅓ cup plus 1 tablespoon
all-purpose flour, sifted
1 tablespoon orange liqueur
vanilla ice cream or crème
fraîche, to serve

· Grease six ⅔ cup metal molds or ramekins and place
on a baking sheet. Melt the chocolate in a heatproof
bowl set over a saucepan of gently simmering water,
then add the orange rind, reserving a few strands for
decoration. Once the chocolate has melted, stir until
smooth, then let cool slightly.

· Place the butter, sugar, eggs, flour, and liqueur in a
food processor or blender and blend to form a smooth
batter. Add the melted chocolate and process again
until well combined.

· Pour the batter into the prepared dishes and place in a
preheated oven, at 375°F, for 9 minutes. The outside should
be cooked, with a molten center. Serve immediately with
scoops of vanilla ice cream or crème fraîche and decorate
with the reserved orange rind.

Chocolate Orange Liqueur Sauce

Place 8 oz semisweet dark
chocolate, broken into small
pieces, in a heatproof bowl,
then pour over ½ cup warmed
light cream. Stir until the
chocolate has melted, then
stir in 1 tablespoon orange
liqueur. Serve the warm sauce
poured over vanilla ice cream.

Chocolate Orange Tart

Melt 8 oz bittersweet dark
chocolate (85 percent cocoa
solids), broken into small pieces,
in a heatproof bowl set over a
saucepan of gently simmering
water, stirring occasionally, then
let cool slightly. Meanwhile,
place 2 extra-large eggs, ¼ cup
superfine sugar, and the grated
rind of 1 orange in a bowl and
beat with a handheld electric
mixer until pale and fluffy.
Beat in the chocolate and
1 tablespoon orange liqueur

until well combined, then
stir in ½ cup heavy cream.
Place an 8 inch store-bought
piecrust on a baking sheet. Pour
in the chocolate mixture and
spread the top level. Place in a
preheated oven, at 325°F, for
about 10–12 minutes or until
just set. The mixture should be
slightly wobbly in the center, but
will continue to set on cooling.
Let cool for 10 minutes, then
serve warm with spoonfuls of
crème fraîche.

 Chocolate Risotto

Serves 4

2½ cups milk
2 tablespoons superfine sugar
grated rind of 1 orange
2 tablespoons unsalted butter
⅔ cup risotto rice
4 oz semisweet dark chocolate,
  chopped into small pieces
1–2 tablespoons of brandy
  or orange liqueur (optional)
¼ cup chopped hazelnuts,
  toasted, to serve

- Place the milk and sugar in a saucepan and bring to a simmer, along with the majority of the orange rind (reserve a few pieces for decoration).

- Meanwhile, melt the butter in a heavy saucepan, add the rice, and stir to coat the grains. Add a ladleful of the hot milk and stir well. Once most of the milk has been absorbed, add another ladleful.

- Continue until most of the milk has been absorbed and the rice is creamy but slightly al dente—this should take about 15 minutes.

- Stir in most of the chopped chocolate and brandy or orange liqueur, if using. Spoon into 4 bowls and serve immediately, sprinkled with the hazelnuts and a little grated orange rind.

1 **Quick Chocolate and Orange Rice Pudding** Place two 14 oz cans rice pudding in a saucepan, then stir in the grated rind of ½ orange, 2 tablespoons orange juice, and 4 oz chopped semisweet dark chocolate. Heat through, stirring, until the chocolate has melted. Spoon into 4 bowls and serve immediately.

3 **Chocolate Risotto with Pistachio Thins** Place 6 tablespoons softened unsalted butter and ⅔ cup superfine sugar in a bowl and beat with a handheld electric mixer until light and fluffy. Fold in ⅓ cup plus 1 tablespoon all-purpose flour, sifted, then stir in 2 tablespoons milk and ½ cup chopped pistachio nuts. Place 8 teaspoons of the mixture, spaced well apart, onto 2 large baking sheets lined with nonstick parchment paper. Place in a preheated oven, at 400°F, for 5–7 minutes or until golden around the edges. Let firm up slightly, then lift off using a spatula and curl around a rolling pin. Transfer to a wire rack to cool. Make the risotto as above and serve with the pistachio thins.

Pear and Chocolate Crisps

Serves 4

butter, for greasing
two 13 oz cans pear quarters
    in juice, drained
¼ cup packed light brown sugar
grated rind and juice of
    1 unwaxed lemon
¼ cup chocolate chips or chunks
ice cream, to serve (optional)

For the topping

¾ cup all-purpose flour
4 tablespoons unsalted
    butter, diced
¼ cup packed light brown sugar
¼ cup chocolate chips or chunks
⅓ cup chopped hazelnuts,
    toasted

- Grease four 1¼ cup ovenproof dishes or ramekins and place on a baking sheet. Place the pears, sugar, lemon rind and juice, and chocolate in a large bowl and stir together.

- To make the topping, place the flour in a bowl, add the butter, and rub in with the fingertips until the mixture resembles fine bread crumbs. Alternatively, use a food processor. Stir in the sugar, chocolate, and hazelnuts.

- Spoon the pear mixture into the prepared dishes or ramekins, spooning over any juice. Sprinkle over the topping and press down lightly.

- Place in a preheated oven, at 350°F), for 15 minutes or until golden and bubbling. Serve with spoonfuls of ice cream, if using.

Pears in Hot Chocolate Sauce

Peel, halve, and core 4 pears, then cut into slices. Arrange in 4 serving dishes and sprinkle over the juice of 1 lemon. To make the chocolate sauce, place 4 oz semisweet dark chocolate, broken into small pieces, 2 tablespoons unsalted butter, 2 tablespoons light corn syrup, 2 tablespoons heavy cream, and 3 tablespoons water in a saucepan. Heat gently, stirring until smooth. Spoon over the pears, sprinkle with ¼ cup chopped, toasted hazlenuts, and serve immediately.

Rosemary Poached Pears with Chocolate Sauce

Place 1¼ cups water, ¾ cup superfine sugar, and 3 rosemary sprigs in a saucepan and heat gently until the sugar has dissolved, then bring to a boil. Peel 4 pears, then place the whole pears in the syrup. Cover and simmer for 20–25 minutes until tender, turning the pears occasionally. Remove the pears and place in a serving bowl. Boil the syrup for 2 minutes until thick. Place 7 oz semisweet dark chocolate, broken into small pieces, in a heatproof bowl and pour over ⅔ cup warmed heavy cream. Stir until melted. Serve the pears with the strained syrup and sauce.

DES-HEAV-ZAS

Banana and Chili Chocolate Chimichangas

Serves 6

2 tablespoons superfine sugar
1 teaspoon ground cinnamon
6 ripe bananas, thickly sliced
6 soft tortilla wraps
6 oz chili-flavored dark chocolate, coarsely chopped
2 tablespoons sunflower oil
vanilla ice cream, to serve (optional)

- Mix together the sugar and cinnamon in a small bowl.

- Place some of the banana slices in the center of 1 tortilla, then sprinkle over one-sixth of the chocolate. Fold over the edges of the tortilla to meet in the middle. Then roll over, from the side nearest to you. Place fold side down on a baking sheet. Brush with a little oil, then sprinkle over the cinnamon sugar. Repeat with the remaining ingredients to make 6 chimichangas.

- Place in a preheated oven, at 350°F, for 10 minutes or until golden. Serve immediately with scoops of vanilla ice cream, if using.

1 Mexican Chocolate and Chili Fondue

Place ⅔ cup heavy cream in a saucepan and heat gently. Stir in 8 oz chopped semisweet dark chocolate, 1 seeded and chopped red chili, and ½ teaspoon chili powder. Stir over low heat until the chocolate has melted. Pour into a warm dish and serve with sliced bananas and warm tortilla strips.

3 Warm Chili Chocolate Pudding

Place 5 oz chili-flavored dark chocolate, 2 tablespoons butter, and 3 tablespoons light corn syrup in a saucepan and cook over a gentle heat, stirring occasionally, until melted, then stir in 3 tablespoons heavy cream. Pour into a lightly greased 1 quart ovenproof dish. Place 8 tablespoons (1 stick) softened unsalted butter and ⅔ cup superfine sugar in a bowl and beat together with a handheld electric mixer until light and fluffy. Gradually beat in 2 eggs, then fold in ¾ cup plus 1 tablespoon self-rising flour, sifted, ¼ cup unsweetened cocoa powder, sifted, 1 teaspoon crushed red pepper, and 2 tablespoons milk. Spoon the mixture over the sauce and place in a preheated oven, at 350°F, for 18–20 minutes.

DES-HEAV-ZOI

 Chocolate Pancakes

Serves 4

¾ cup all-purpose flour
1 tablespoon unsweetened
  cocoa powder
pinch of salt
2 eggs, beaten
1¼ cups milk
2 tablespoons unsalted butter,
  melted, plus pat of unsalted
  butter, for frying
7½ oz prepared red fruit compote

For the chocolate sauce

6 oz milk chocolate, broken into
  small pieces
4 tablespoons unsalted butter
2 tablespoons light corn syrup
½ cup milk

- Sift the flour, cocoa powder, and salt into a bowl and make a well in the center. Pour the eggs into the well, then gradually beat into the flour mixture. Add the milk a little at a time, beating to form a smooth batter. Stir in the melted butter.

- To make the chocolate sauce, gently melt the chocolate, butter, and light corn syrup in a saucepan over low heat. Stir in the milk and cook for 2–3 minutes until the sauce thickens, stirring frequently.

- Heat a little of the butter for frying in an 8 inch nonstick crepe pan or skillet. Add a ladleful of batter and swirl to coat the bottom of the pan. Cook for 1–2 minutes until golden, then flip over and cook for an additional 1 minute. Remove from the pan and keep warm. Repeat with the remaining batter to make 8 pancakes, adding more butter if necessary.

- To serve, fill each pancake with a little of the compote and drizzle with the chocolate sauce. Serve 2 per person.

Pancakes with Praline Chocolate

Sauce Melt 8 oz semisweet dark chocolate with honey and praline nougat, finely chopped, in a heatproof bowl set over a saucepan of gently simmering water until completely soft. Do not overstir. Add 2 tablespoons unsalted butter and stir until melted, then stir in ½ cup heavy whipping cream. Meanwhile, heat through 8 store-bought pancakes according to the package directions and serve 2 per person drizzled with the chocolate sauce.

Chocolate and Raspberry Clafoutis

Place 7 tablespoons softened unsalted butter, ⅔ cup superfine sugar, ¾ cup plus 1 tablespoon self-rising flour, sifted, ¼ cup unsweetened cocoa powder, sifted, 3 eggs, and 3 tablespoons milk in a food processor or blender and blend until smooth. Spoon the mixture into four 1 cup greased ovenproof dishes, then divide 1 cup raspberries among them. Place on a baking sheet and bake in a preheated oven, at 375°F, for 15–16 minutes until risen and set.

30 White Chocolate, Lemon Grass, and Cardamom Mousse

Serves 6

½ cup milk

2 lemon grass stalks,
  coarsely chopped

8 oz white chocolate
  (30 percent cocoa solids),
  broken into small pieces

crushed seeds from 4 green
  cardamom pods

1 cup mascarpone cheese

3 egg whites

white chocolate curls, to serve

unsweetened cocoa powder,
  for dusting

- Place 6 small ramekins in a freezer. Pour the milk into a small saucepan and add the lemon grass. Bring to a boil, then remove from the heat and let stand and steep for 5 minutes.

- Meanwhile, melt together the chocolate and crushed cardamom seeds in a heatproof bowl set over a saucepan of gently simmering water, stirring occasionally. Remove from the heat.

- Strain the warm milk into the melted chocolate and stir well. Beat in the mascarpone with a handheld electric mixer until smooth, then chill.

- Beat the egg whites in a clean bowl with a handheld electric mixer until stiff, then gently fold into the chocolate mixture. Spoon into the ramekins and place in the freezer for 5–10 minutes before serving. Alternatively, to make ahead, cover and chill in the refrigerator until required.

- Top with white chocolate curls and dust with unsweetened cocoa powder and serve.

 Speedy White Chocolate, Lemon Grass, and Cardamom Sauce Place 2 chopped lemon grass stalks, 4 crushed cardamom pods, and ½ cup milk in a saucepan and bring to a boil, then remove from the heat and let steep for 5 minutes. Meanwhile, melt 8 oz white chocolate, broken into small pieces, in a heatproof bowl set over a saucepan of gently simmering water, then strain over the milk and stir well. Serve immediately on ice cream or fruit.

White Chocolate, Lemon Grass, and Cardamom Tart Place 2 chopped lemon grass stalks and ½ cup milk in a saucepan and bring to a boil. Remove from the heat and let steep for 5 minutes. Meanwhile melt 7 oz white chocolate (30 percent cocoa solids) in a heatproof bowl set over a pan of simmering water, stirring occasionally. Strain the warm milk into the chocolate and add the crushed seeds of 4 green cardamom pods. Beat together 2 cups mascarpone cheese and 3 tablespoons confectioners' sugar, then whisk in the chocolate mixture. Spoon the filling into an 8 inch store-bought piecrust. Chill until ready to serve.

Chocolate Sorbet Bites

Serves 4

8 oz frozen mango or raspberry sorbet

5 oz semisweet dark chocolate, broken into small pieces

To decorate (optional)

chopped nuts

dried raspberry flakes

chocolate sprinkles

- Line a large baking sheet with nonstick parchment paper and place in the freezer, set on its lowest setting, for 5 minutes.

- Using a melon baller, shape the sorbet into about 16 balls and place on the baking sheet. Insert a toothpick into each ball, then place in the freezer.

- Melt the chocolate in a heatproof bowl set over a saucepan of gently simmering water, stirring occasionally. Let cool to room temperature. One by one, dip the sorbet balls into the chocolate so they are completely coated.

- Decorate, if liked, with chopped nuts, raspberry flakes, and chocolate sprinkles and return to the freezer for at least 10 minutes.

- Remove from the freezer 5 minutes before serving.

Ice Cream Cookie Choc Ices

Melt 2 oz semisweet dark chocolate, broken into small pieces, in a heatproof bowl set over a saucepan of gently simmering water. Brush the melted chocolate onto one side of 8 vanilla-flavored cookies. Cut 4 thick slices of ice cream, the same size as the cookies, and place on the chocolate sides of 4 cookies. Sandwich together with the remaining cookies, chocolate side down, and serve immediately.

Chocolate Cones

Melt 6 oz semisweet dark chocolate, broken into small pieces, in a heatproof bowl set over a saucepan of gently simmering water. Dip the ends of 4 waffle ice cream cones into the melted chocolate, then stand in glasses and pour the remaining chocolate into the bottom of each cone. Chill for 10 minutes until set. Add a little chopped fresh fruit to the bottom of the cones, then top with sorbet or ice cream. Serve immediately.

DES-HEAV-NYB

30 White Chocolate and Strawberry Cheesecake

Serves 6–8

1¼ cups crushed Graham crackers

6 tablespoons unsalted butter, melted

8 oz white chocolate (30 percent cocoa solids), broken into small pieces

2 cups mascarpone cheese

3 tablespoons confectioners' sugar, sifted

1¼ cups hulled and sliced strawberries

grated white chocolate, to decorate

- Stir the crushed crackers into the melted butter and press into the bottom of an 8 inch, loose-bottom, round cake pan. Chill while you make the filling.

- Melt the chocolate in a heatproof bowl set over a saucepan of gently simmering water, stirring occasionally.

- Place the mascarpone in a bowl and beat in the confectioners' sugar until smooth. Beat in the chocolate, then spread the mixture over the cheesecake base.

- Chill for 15 minutes, then arrange the strawberries over the top and decorate with the grated chocolate. Serve immediately or chill until ready to serve.

---

1 Strawberries with Warm White Chocolate Sauce

Hull and halve 1 lb 5 oz strawberries and divide among 6 glasses. Warm 1¾ cups heavy cream in a small saucepan. Remove from the heat and stir in 6 oz chopped white chocolate. Stir until melted, then pour over the strawberries. Serve immediately.

2 Individual White Chocolate and Strawberry Cheesecakes

Divide 6 crushed Graham crackers among 6 small glasses. Place 2 cups hulled and chopped strawberries in a bowl and sprinkle with 1 tablespoon confectioners' sugar. Meanwhile, melt 4 oz white chocolate (30 per cent cocoa solids), broken into small pieces, in a heatproof bowl set over a saucepan of gently simmering water, then let cool slightly. Place 1 cup mascarpone cheese, ¼ cup heavy cream, and 1 tablespoon confectioners' sugar in a large bowl and beat in the melted chocolate. Spoon into the glasses, then top with the strawberries. Chill until ready to serve.

2 Chocolate and Cherry Trifle

Serves 6–8

3 oz semisweet dark chocolate, broken into small pieces

1¾ cups vanilla pudding or custard (see page 150)

13 oz store-bought chocolate jelly roll, cut into ½ inch thick slices

⅓ cup cherry conserve or jam

¼ cup kirsch

3 cups halved and pitted cherries, plus extra to decorate

2 cups heavy whipping cream

chocolate curls, to decorate

· Melt the chocolate in a heatproof bowl set over a saucepan of gently simmering water, then let cool. Place the pudding in a bowl and beat in the melted chocolate.

· Line the sides and bottom of an 8 inch diameter bowl with the jelly roll. Mix together the conserve and kirsch in a bowl, then spoon over the cake. Scatter the cherries over the top and spoon over the chocolate pudding.

· Lightly whip the cream in a bowl with a handheld electric mixer until it forms soft peaks, then spoon over the pudding. Decorate with chocolate curls and a few extra cherries. Serve immediately or chill until ready to serve.

---

1 Quick Chocolate Cherry Puddings

Cut a store-bought chocolate jelly roll into six ¾ inch thick slices and place in 6 bowls. Spoon 1 tablespoon kirsch, taken from a jar of cherries in kirsch, over each, then spoon 4 of the cherries from the jar into each bowl. Place 1½ cups store-bought vanilla pudding or custard (see page 150) in a saucepan and heat gently, stir in 2 oz chopped semisweet dark chocolate, and stir until melted. Serve poured over the puddings.

3 Chocolate and Cherry Tart

Put ⅔ cup cream cheese, ½ cup heavy cream, 2 tablespoons unsweetened cocoa powder, sifted, 3 tablespoons superfine sugar, and 2 egg yolks in a bowl and beat together. Spoon into an 8 inch store-bought piecrust. Drain a 14 oz can pitted black cherries and arrange over the chocolate mixture. Place in a preheated oven, at 350°F, for 18–20 minutes or until set.

3⦿ Spiced Chocolate Sponge with Chocolate Sauce

Serves 4–6

8 tablespoons (1 stick) unsalted butter, cut into pieces, plus extra for greasing

1 cup store-bought chocolate sauce

4 oz semisweet dark chocolate, broken into small pieces

½ cup packed light brown sugar

1 cup self-rising flour

1 teaspoon ground cinnamon

½ teaspoon ground nutmeg

¼ teaspoon ground cloves

2 eggs, beaten

2 tablespoons milk

light cream, to serve (optional)

- Lightly grease a 1 quart ovenproof dish, then pour the chocolate sauce in the bottom.

- Melt together the butter and chocolate in a heatproof bowl set over a saucepan of gently simmering water, then stir in the sugar.

- Sift the flour and spices into a large bowl, then pour in the chocolate mixture, eggs, and milk and mix well.

- Spoon the mixture over the sauce (if it sinks, don't worry; it will rise on cooking) and place in a preheated oven, at 350°F, for 20–25 minutes or until risen and bubbling.

- Let cool in the dish for a few minutes, then serve with light cream, if using.

1⦿ Quick Spiced Chocolate Sauce

Gently warm through 1 cup store-bought chocolate sauce in a saucepan and stir in 1 teaspoon ground cinnamon along with ¼ teaspoon each of ground cloves and nutmeg. Serve poured over vanilla ice cream.

2⦿ Individual Spiced Melting Chocolate Puddings Melt together 6 oz semisweet dark chocolate (70 percent cocoa solids), broken into small pieces, and 12 tablespoons (1½ sticks) diced unsalted butter in a heatproof bowl set over a saucepan of gently simmering water, stirring occasionally. Place 3 eggs, plus 3 egg yolks and ⅓ cup superfine sugar, in a bowl and beat with a handheld electric mixer until thick and foamy. Beat in the melted chocolate, then sift in heaping 3 teaspoons all-purpose flour, ½ teaspoon ground cinnamon, and ¼ teaspoon each ground cloves and nutmeg. Spoon the mixture into six ¾ cup greased ramekins or metal molds, their bottoms lined with nonstick parchment paper. Place on a baking sheet and bake in a preheated oven, at 425°F, for 10 minutes or until set but still soft in the centers. Turn out the puddings onto serving plates and serve immediately.

 Chocolate and Ginger Tart

Serves 6–8

8 oz semisweet dark chocolate
(85% cocoa solids), broken into
small pieces
2 extra-large eggs
¼ cup superfine sugar
2 pieces of preserved ginger in
syrup, finely chopped
½ cup heavy cream
8 inch store-bought piecrust
unsweetened cocoa powder,
for dusting
vanilla ice cream or crème
fraîche, to serve (optional)

- Melt the chocolate in a heatproof bowl set over a saucepan of gently simmering water, stirring occasionally, then let cool slightly.

- Place the eggs and sugar in a bowl and beat with a handheld electric mixer until pale and fluffy. Beat in the melted chocolate until well combined, then stir in the preserved ginger and cream.

- Place the piecrust on a baking sheet. Pour in the chocolate mixture and spread the top level. Place in a preheated oven, at 325° F, for about 10–12 minutes or until just set. The mixture should be slightly wobbly in the center, but will continue to set on cooling.

- Dust with cocoa powder. Serve warm or cold with a scoop of vanilla ice cream or crème fraîche, if using.

---

1 **Chocolate and Ginger Sauce**

Melt together 8 oz semisweet dark chocolate, broken into small pieces, 1¼ cups heavy cream, 2 pieces of preserved ginger in syrup, finely chopped, and 2 tablespoons preserved ginger syrup in a saucepan over low heat. Cook until melted and smooth and shiny, stirring occasionally. Serve the sauce over vanilla ice cream or bananas.

2 **Chocolate and Ginger Mousses**

Melt together 5 oz semisweet dark chocolate, broken into small pieces, and 2 pieces of preserved ginger in syrup, finely chopped, in a heatproof bowl set over a saucepan of gently simmering water. Meanwhile, whip ½ cup heavy cream in a bowl using a handheld electric mixer until it forms soft peaks. Fold the chocolate mixture, a little at a time, into the cream. Beat 2 egg whites in a clean bowl with a handheld electric mixer until stiff, then gently fold into the chocolate cream. Spoon into 6 small espresso cups or ramekins and chill for 10 minutes.

 # Chocolate and Pistachio Soufflés

Serves 6

butter, for greasing
¼ cup pistachio nuts, ground
5 oz semisweet dark chocolate
(72 percent cocoa solids),
broken into small pieces
4 eggs, separated
½ cup superfine sugar
2 teaspoons cornstarch
unsweetened cocoa powder
or confectioners' sugar,
for dusting (optional)

- Grease six ¾ cup ramekins, then lightly dust with 1 tablespoon of the ground pistachios to cover the bottom and sides. (This helps the soufflés to rise.) Place on a baking sheet.

- Melt the chocolate in a heatproof bowl set over a saucepan of gently simmering water, then let cool slightly.

- Meanwhile, beat the egg whites in a clean large bowl with a handheld electric mixer until stiff, then gradually beat in half the sugar until the mixture is thick and glossy.

- Stir the remaining sugar, egg yolks, and cornstarch into the cooled chocolate mixture. Gently fold some of the egg white mixture into the chocolate mixture, then gently fold in the remainder, with the remaining pistachios. Spoon into the prepared dishes and spread the tops level, then clean the edges with a fingertip.

- Place in a preheated oven, at 375°F, for 20 minutes or until risen. Dust with cocoa powder or confectioners' sugar, if using, and serve immediately.

---

1 Pistachio and Choc Chip Freeze

Place 1 lb 3½ oz pistachio ice cream and ⅔ cup milk chocolate chips in a food processor and process until just combined. Spoon into 6 small glasses. Scatter over ¼ cup chopped pistachios and serve immediately with thin vanilla cookies on the side.

2 Pistachio Chocolate Brownie Puddings

Place 6 tablespoons softened unsalted butter, ½ cup packed light brown sugar, and 1 teaspoon vanilla extract in a bowl and beat with a handheld electric mixer until light and fluffy. Add ¼ cup unsweetened cocoa powder, sifted, ⅓ cup plus 1 tablespoon self-rising flour, sifted, and 1 egg and beat until combined. Stir in ½ cup chopped pistachios. Spoon the mixture into a lightly greased 6-cup nonstick muffin pan, and place in a preheated oven, at 350°F, for 10–12 minutes or until just cooked but still soft in the centers. Turn out the puddings onto serving plates and serve immediately with heavy cream or crème fraîche.

DES-HEAV-MUX

Apricot, Chocolate and Brioche Tart

Serves 6–8

butter, for greasing
8 oz brioche loaf, cut into
½ inch slices
½ cup milk or semisweet dark
chocolate drops or chunks
1 extra-large egg
2 tablespoons superfine sugar
1 cup mascarpone cheese
two 13 oz cans apricot halves,
drained
3 tablespoons Demerara sugar

- Lightly grease a shallow, rectangular tart pan, about 12 x 8 inch. Arrange the brioche slices in the bottom, cutting them to fit where necessary and filling any gaps with the bread. Scatter over half the chocolate.

- Lightly beat together the egg, superfine sugar, and mascarpone in a bowl until smooth, then spoon over the bread, leaving a ½ inch border. Scatter over the remaining chocolate.

- Arrange the apricots in neat lines, cut side up, over the mascarpone mixture and sprinkle with the Demerara sugar.

- Place in a preheated oven, at 350°F, for 20–25 minutes or until the custard is set. Serve in slices.

---

1 **Apricot Brioche Toasts with Chocolate Sauce** Lightly toast 6 thick slices of brioche, place on 6 serving plates, and top each with 1 apricot, halved and pitted. Meanwhile, melt 5 oz semisweet dark chocolate, broken into small pieces, 2 tablespoons orange liqueur, and ¼ cup heavy cream in a heatproof bowl set over a saucepan of gently simmering water. Pour over the apricot toasts and serve immediately.

2 **Chocolate Brioche with Apricots** Beat together 2 eggs, 1 cup milk, and 2 tablespoons superfine sugar in a shallow dish. Add 6 slices of chocolate brioche, each cut in half, and turn to coat. Melt together 2 tablespoons unsalted butter and 2 tablespoons superfine sugar in a skillet, add 14½ oz halved and pitted apricots, and cook gently for 5 minutes until the apricots have softened and released their juice. Melt

2 tablespoons unsalted butter in a large skillet and add the brioche. Cook for 2 minutes on each side or until golden brown, then serve 2 slices per person topped with the apricots and their juice and a scoop of vanilla ice cream.

3 Fruity Chocolate Bread and Butter Pudding

Serves 4

2 tablespoons unsalted
butter, softened, plus
extra for greasing
4 oz milk chocolate,
broken into small pieces
12 slices of fruit loaf
1¾ cups store-bought
vanilla pudding or custard
(see page 150)
½ cup milk
3 tablespoons golden raisins
2 tablespoons Demerara sugar

- Grease a 1 quart ovenproof dish. Melt the chocolate in a heatproof bowl set over a saucepan of gently simmering water. Meanwhile, butter each slice of bread, then cut in half diagonally, forming triangles.

- Place the vanilla pudding in a pitcher and stir in the melted chocolate. Mix in the milk.

- Arrange a layer of bread in the bottom of the prepared dish. Sprinkle with the golden raisins, then place the remaining bread on top. Pour over the chocolate pudding and let stand for 5 minutes.

- Sprinkle with the sugar and place in a preheated oven, at 350°F, for 20 minutes or until bubbling.

---

1 Fruity Chocolate Cinnamon Bread

Beat together 2 extra-large eggs and 3 tablespoons milk in a shallow dish. Spread 2 slices of fruit bread with 2 tablespoons chocolate spread, then place another 2 slices of bread on top. Add to the egg mixture and let stand for 1 minute, then turn to coat. Melt a pat of unsalted butter and 1 tablespoon oil in a skillet and cook the bread slices on each side for 3–4 minutes until golden. Cut in half, place on 4 serving plates, and serve sprinkled with 2 tablespoons superfine sugar mixed with 1 teaspoon ground cinnamon.

2 Individual Chocolate and Orange Bread Puddings

Spread 12 slices of fruit bread with 2 tablespoons softened unsalted butter and cut into triangles. Arrange 1 layer of the bread in the bottom of 4 lightly greased 1 cup ovenproof dishes. Mix together 1¾ cups freshly prepared chocolate pudding with the grated rind of 1 orange and 2 tablespoons orange juice. Pour half over the bread. Repeat until all the ingredients are used up. Sprinkle with 2 tablespoons Demerara sugar. Place on a baking sheet and bake in a preheated oven,

at 350°F, for 15 minutes or until bubbling.

3 Gooey Chocolate and Prune Torte

Serves 8

5 oz semisweet dark chocolate
  (70 percent cocoa solids),
  broken into small pieces
¼ cup brandy
1 cup prunes, coarsely chopped
7 tablespoons unsalted butter,
  diced
4 eggs, separated
½ cup superfine sugar
⅓ cup plus 1 tablespoon
  all-purpose flour
1 teaspoon baking powder
whipped cream, to serve
unsweetened cocoa powder,
  for dusting

- Line the bottom of an 8 inch round springform cake pan with nonstick parchment paper. Melt together the chocolate, brandy, prunes, and butter in a heatproof bowl set over a saucepan of gently simmering water.

- Meanwhile, place the egg yolks and sugar in a bowl and beat with a handheld electric mixer until pale and thick and the beaters leaves a trail when lifted above the mixture. Fold in the flour and baking powder. Add the melted chocolate mixture, stirring gently to combine.

- Beat the egg whites until stiff in a clean, large bowl with a handheld electric mixer, then lightly fold into the chocolate mixture.

- Spoon into the prepared pan and place in a preheated oven, at 350°F, for 20 minutes or until risen and set on top, but still soft in the center. Let cool in the pan for a few minutes.

- Place the torte on a serving plate and serve immediately with whipped cream and a dusting of cocoa powder.

---

1 Chocolate-Coated Prunes

Melt 6 oz semisweet dark chocolate, broken into small pieces, in a heatproof bowl set over a saucepan of gently simmering water, then remove from the heat. Using a fork, dip 1¾ cups pitted prunes into the chocolate. Place on a baking sheet lined with nonstick parchment paper and chill for 5–8 minutes until set. Serve dusted with unsweetened cocoa powder.

2 Chocolate and Prune Refrigerator

Bars Melt 8 oz semisweet dark chocolate (at least 70 percent cocoa solids), broken into small pieces, in a heatproof bowl set over a saucepan of gently simmering water, then stir in 4 tablespoons unsalted butter. Using a rolling pin, roughly smash 18 Graham crackers into small pieces and stir into the chocolate mixture with 1 cup chopped prunes. Spoon the mixture into an 8 inch square cake pan lined with nonstick parchment paper and place in the freezer for 10 minutes to set. Using a sharp knife, cut into 12 bars. Store any leftover bars in an airtight container for up to 3–4 days.

Chocolate Mousse with Honeycomb Toffee

Serves 6

8 oz semisweet dark chocolate, broken into small pieces

4 eggs, separated

⅔ cup heavy cream

For the honeycomb toffee

sunflower oil, for greasing

⅓ cup granulated sugar

2 tablespoons light corn syrup

1 teaspoon baking soda

- To make the honeycomb toffee, oil a baking sheet and set on a cutting board. Gently heat the sugar and light corn syrup in a heavy saucepan until the sugar has dissolved, then boil until the mixture turns a deep golden caramel. Beat in the baking soda (this will make it foam up), then quickly pour it onto the prepared baking sheet and let cool for 10 minutes.

- Meanwhile, melt the chocolate in a heatproof bowl set over a saucepan of gently simmering water. Let cool slightly, then stir in the egg yolks. Lightly whip the cream in a bowl with a handheld electric mixer until it forms soft peaks and fold into the chocolate mixture.

- Beat the egg whites in a clean large bowl with a handheld electric mixer until stiff, then fold into the chocolate cream.

- Break the honeycomb toffee into small chunks and fold most of it into the mousse. Pour into 6 glasses or individual dishes and chill for 10 minutes until set. Sprinkle the leftover honeycomb toffee over the top just before serving.

1 Easy Crunchy Chocolate Honeycomb Toffee Ice Cream Place 2 large scoops of vanilla ice cream into each of 6 bowls. Roughly break up two 1¾ oz bars chocolate honeycomb toffee (sponge candy) and sprinkle over the ice cream. Drizzle each with 2 tablespoons warmed store-bought chocolate sauce and serve immediately.

2 Speedy Chocolate and Honeycomb Toffee Pots Melt 5 oz milk chocolate, broken into small pieces, in a heatproof bowl set over a saucepan of gently simmering water, then stir in two 1¾ oz crumbled chocolate honeycomb toffee (sponge candy) bars. Gently beat together 1¼ cups heavy cream and 1 cup mascarpone cheese in a bowl and fold in the chocolate mixture. Spoon into 6 small glasses and chill for 10 minutes. Serve with extra grated chocolate.

QuickCook

Family
Favorites

Recipes listed by cooking time

Banana-Caramel Pie

Serves 6–8

2⅓ cups crushed Graham crackers or gingersnaps

7½ tablespoons unsalted butter, melted

⅔ cup heavy whipping cream

3 small bananas

13 oz can dulce de leche (thick caramel)

grated chocolate, to decorate

- Stir the crushed cookies into the melted butter and press into the bottom and sides of a 7½ inch loose-bottom tart pan. Chill for 15 minutes.

- Meanwhile, lightly whip the cream in a bowl with a handheld electric mixer until it forms soft peaks. Slice the bananas.

- Spread the dulce de leche over the cookie base and top with most of the banana slices, reserving a few for decoration.

- Cover with the whipped cream and decorate with the remaining bananas and grated chocolate. Serve immediately or chill until ready to serve.

Banana-Caramel Ice Cream Sundaes

Crumble 6 gingersnaps and place in the bottom of 6 tall sundae glasses. Slice 6 bananas and arrange half over the top of the cookies. Add 1 scoop of vanilla ice cream to each glass, then drizzle with 2 tablespoons warmed store-bought caramel sauce. Add the remaining bananas and another scoop of ice cream to each, top with more caramel sauce, and serve immediately.

Banana-Caramel Fools

Crush 8 gingersnaps and mix with 2 tablespoons melted unsalted butter. Slice 3 large bananas and place in a bowl. Sprinkle with 1 tablespoon lemon juice, then stir in 7 tablespoons dulce de leche (thick caramel). Lightly whip 1 cup heavy cream in a bowl with a handheld electric mixer until it forms soft peaks, then fold in 1 cup prepared vanilla pudding. Spoon 1 tablespoon of the cookie crumbs into each of 6 glasses, spoon over half the banana-caramel mixture and half the vanilla pudding mixture. Repeat the layers, then top with a little grated chocolate. Serve immediately.

Blueberry Pancakes

Serves 4

1¼ cups all-purpose flour
1 teaspoon baking powder
pinch of salt
2 tablespoons superfine sugar
⅔ cup milk
2 tablespoons unsalted
   butter, melted
1 egg
½ teaspoon vanilla extract
pat of unsalted butter,
   for frying
1 cup blueberries

To serve

maple syrup or honey
vanilla ice cream

- Sift the flour, baking powder, and salt into a bowl. Stir in the sugar and make a well in the center. Whisk together the milk, melted butter, egg, and vanilla extract in a pitcher, then gradually beat into the flour to form a smooth batter.

- Heat a little of the butter for frying in a large skillet over medium heat. Add heaping tablespoons of the batter mixture to make pancakes about 3½–4 inches in diameter.

- Scatter the blueberries over the top of the batter and cook for 2–3 minutes until bubbles start to appear on the surface, then flip over and cook for an additional 1–2 minutes. Remove from the skillet and keep warm. Repeat with the remaining batter to make 8–10 pancakes, adding a little more butter to the skillet and reducing the heat if necessary.

- Serve the pancakes drizzled with maple syrup or honey, with a scoop of ice cream on top.

---

1 **Blueberry Compote**

Place 1⅓ cups blueberries, 2 tablespoons superfine sugar, and 1 tablespoon lemon juice in a saucepan and heat gently, stirring occasionally, until the blueberries start to pop and release their juices. Simmer for 3–4 minutes until jammy. Delicious served poured over warmed store-bought pancakes or ice cream.

3 **Blueberry Batter Puddings**

Sift ⅔ cup all-purpose flour and a pinch of salt into a bowl. Stir in ¼ cup superfine sugar and make a well in the center. Whisk together 1 cup milk, 1 teaspoon vanilla extract, and 2 extra-large eggs in a pitcher, then gradually whisk into the flour to form a smooth batter. Pour into a lightly greased 12-hole muffin pan, then divide 1 cup blueberries among the puddings, placing them in the center of each one. Place in a preheated oven, at 350°F, for 20 minutes or until risen, golden, and cooked through. Serve 3 per person, dusted with confectioners' sugar.

 **Strawberry with Meringues**

Serves 6

3 cups hulled and chopped strawberries

2 teaspoons confectioners' sugar

2 cups heavy cream

8 meringue nests, broken into 1 inch pieces

- Place half the strawberries and the confectioners' sugar in a food processor or blender and blend to form a puree.

- Lightly whip the cream in a large bowl with a handheld electric mixer until it forms soft peaks, then fold in the meringue nests and remaining strawberries. Swirl in half the puree.

- Spoon into 4 glasses, drizzle with the remaining puree, and serve immediately.

---

2 **Meringues with Strawberry Cream**

Place 5 oz hulled strawberries and 1 tablespoon confectioners' sugar in a food processor or blender and blend to form a puree. Lightly whip 1 cup heavy cream in a bowl with a handheld electric mixer until it forms soft peaks, then stir in the strawberry puree. Spoon into 6 meringue nests and decorate each with a strawberry. Chill for 10 minutes before serving.

3 **Baked Strawberry Meringue Pie**

Roll out 11 oz chilled, store-bought basic pastry dough on a lightly floured surface and use to line a 9 inch loose-bottom tart pan, then prick the bottom with a fork. Line with nonstick parchment paper and pie weights or dried beans and bake in a preheated oven, at 1375°F, for 10 minutes. Remove the paper and weights and return to the oven for an additional 5 minutes or until golden. Spread the bottom of the piecrust with 2 tablespoons strawberry jam, then arrange 12 oz hulled and halved strawberries over the jam. Whisk 4 egg whites in a clean, large bowl with a handheld electric mixer until stiff, then gradually whisk in 1 cup superfine sugar until the mixture is thick and glossy. Pile on top of the pie, then place in the oven for 8–10 minutes or until the meringue is golden.

Lemon and Ricotta Pancakes

Serves 4

1 cup ricotta cheese
½ cup milk
3 eggs, separated
grated rind and juice of
  1 unwaxed lemon
¾ cup all-purpose flour
1 teaspoon baking powder
pinch of salt
3 tablespoons superfine sugar,
  plus extra for sprinkling
pat of unsalted butter,
  for frying

- Place the ricotta, milk, egg yolks, and lemon rind in a large bowl and beat together. Stir in the flour, baking powder, salt, and sugar.

- Whisk the egg whites in a clean, large bowl with a handheld electric mixer until stiff, then gently fold into the ricotta mixture.

- Heat a little of the butter in a large skillet over medium heat and add tablespoons of batter to form pancakes about 3 inches in diameter. Cook for 1–2 minutes on each side until golden brown. Remove from the skillet and keep warm. Repeat with the remaining batter to make 24 pancakes, adding more butter and reducing the heat if necessary.

- Serve a small stack of pancakes on each of 4 plates, drizzled with the lemon juice and sprinkled with superfine sugar.

---

1 Quick Lemon Pancakes

Warm through 8 store-bought pancakes according to the package directions. Sprinkle with superfine sugar and lemon juice, to taste, and serve 2 pancakes per person with wedges of lemon.

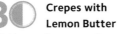

3 Crepes with Lemon Butter

Sift ¾ cup all-purpose flour and a pinch of salt into a large bowl and make a well in the center. Pour 2 beaten eggs into the well, then gradually beat into the flour. Add 1¼ cups milk a little at a time, beating to form a smooth batter. Stir in 2 tablespoons melted unsalted butter. To make the lemon butter, place 8 tablespoons (1 stick) unsalted softened butter, 1 cup confectioners' sugar, and the grated rind of 1 unwaxed lemon in a bowl and beat together with a handheld electric mixer until light and fluffy. Chill the butter while you make the pancakes. Heat a little unsalted butter in an 8 inch nonstick crepe pan or skillet. Add a ladleful of batter and swirl around to coat the bottom of the pan. Cook for 1–2 minutes until golden, then flip over and cook for an additional minute. Repeat with the remaining batter to make 8 crepes and keep warm. Melt a pat of the lemon butter in the pan and add a little lemon juice. Return a crepe to the foaming butter and heat through. Fold in half and then in quarters. Repeat with the remaining butter and pancakes. Serve 2 pancakes per person on warmed plates.

 # Bananas and Pecans with Butterscotch Custard

Serves 4

½ cup packed light brown sugar

2 tablespoons light corn syrup

4 tablespoons unsalted butter, diced

12 oz can evaporated milk

2 tablespoons instant vanilla pudding mix

2 tablespoons cold water

2 tablespoons rum (optional)

4 large bananas, sliced

½ cup chopped pecans

- Place the sugar, light corn syrup, and butter in a saucepan over medium heat and bring to a boil, stirring occasionally. Pour in 1 cup of the evaporated milk and cook for 3 minutes.

- Place the vanilla pudding mix in medium bowl and stir in the measured water to form a paste, then gradually stir in half the remaining evaporated milk until smooth (use the remaining milk in another recipe). Pour into the hot sauce and cook, stirring continuously, for 2–3 minutes until the custard is thick and smooth. Stir in the rum, if using.

- Arrange the bananas in a dish and sprinkle over the pecans. Pour over the hot custard and serve immediately.

---

2 **Bananas with Butterscotch Sauce**

Melt 5 tablespoons unsalted butter and ½ cup packed dark brown sugar in a large skillet over medium heat. Peel 4 bananas and leave whole. Place in the skillet and cook for 3–4 minutes on each side. Stir in 2 tablespoons rum (optional) and cook for an additional 2–3 minutes. Serve immediately with the sauce and scoops of vanilla ice cream.

3 **Banana and Butterscotch Puddings with Sauce**

Place 1 cup self-rising flour and ½ cup superfine sugar in a bowl, then whisk in 2 mashed bananas, 1 lightly beaten egg, 2 tablespoons light corn syrup, ½ cup milk, and 6½ tablespoons melted unsalted butter. Stir in ½ cup chopped pecans. Pour into 4 greased, 2-cup ovenproof dishes placed on a baking sheet. Place ⅔ cup dark brown sugar, ¼ cup light corn syrup, and 1 cup boiling water in a saucepan and bring to a boil, stirring until the sugar has dissolved. Pour into a pitcher and then pour equally over the puddings. Bake in a preheated oven, at 350°F, for 20–25 minutes.

 # Cinnamon Brioche French Toast with Mixed Berries

Serves 4

1 extra-large egg
1 teaspoon ground cinnamon
2 tablespoons superfine sugar
½ cup milk
pat of unsalted butter, for frying
4 thick slices of brioche bread
3 cups mixed berries,
   such as strawberries,
   raspberries, blueberries,
   and cherries
vanilla ice cream, to serve

- Mix together the egg, cinnamon, and sugar in a shallow dish, then whisk in the milk.

- Heat a large skillet over medium heat and add a little butter. Dip 2 slices of the bread in the egg mixture, then place in the hot skillet. Cook for 2–3 minutes on each side until golden. Remove from the skillet and keep warm. Repeat with the remaining bread, adding a little more butter if necessary.

- Top with the mixed berries and serve with scoops of vanilla ice cream.

2 Cinnamon Brioche French Toast with Mixed Berry Compote

Place 4 cups mixed berries, such as raspberries, hulled and halved strawberries, and blackberries, in a large saucepan with ⅓ cup superfine sugar and 2–3 tablespoons water. Bring to a boil and simmer for about 5 minutes, then let cool for 10 minutes. Meanwhile, make the brioche toast as above. Serve the cooled compote over the brioche toasts.

3 Brioche Mixed Berry Puddings

Make the Mixed Berry Compote (see left). Pour the simmered mixture into a strainer over a bowl, reserving the berries and the juice. Let cool for 10 minutes. Cut 8 slices of brioche and lightly toast. Place 4 pieces of the bread on 4 serving plates and spoon over some of the juice, then some of the berries. Top with the remaining brioche slices, pouring over more juice and berries. Serve immediately with thick heavy cream.

 Warm Marshmallow Dip with Fruit Kebabs

Serves 4

2 cups mixed fruit, such as hulled, small strawberries, sliced bananas, pitted cherries, and raspberries

32 pink and white marshmallows

½ cup light cream

- Thread the fruit onto short bamboo skewers.

- Heat the marshmallows and cream in a nonstick saucepan over low heat, stirring continuously, until the marshmallows have melted. Pour into a warm bowl and serve with the fruit kebabs for dipping.

2 Marshmallow Brochettes with Chocolate Sauce Melt 2 oz semisweet dark chocolate, broken into small pieces, in a heatproof bowl set over a saucepan of gently simmering water. Whisk in 1 tablespoon unsalted butter and 3 tablespoons heavy cream to form a smooth sauce. Thread 28 pink and white marshmallows, alternately, onto eight 5 inch metal skewers, then run over a gas flame or use a chef's blow torch to singe the edges. Serve 2 brochettes per person with the chocolate sauce.

3 Marshmallow Mousse Make the Warm Marshmallow Dip as above and chill for 5 minutes. Meanwhile, whisk 2 egg whites in a clean bowl with a handheld electric mixer until stiff, then gently fold into the marshmallow mixture. Spoon into 4 glasses and chill for 10–15 minutes until set. Serve decorated with mini marshmallows.

 Rocky Road Ice Cream Sundaes

Serves 4

½ cup store-bought hot
chocolate sauce
1 cup small chocolate
chip cookie pieces
16 small scoops of vanilla
ice cream
32 pink and white marshmallows

To serve

a few mini marshmallows
a little grated chocolate

- Place the chocolate sauce in a saucepan over low heat and warm through.

- Meanwhile, place a handful of the cookie pieces in each of 4 tall sundae glasses. Add 2 scoops of vanilla ice cream to each glass. Add 4 of the marshmallows to each sundae, then spoon 1 tablespoon of the warm chocolate sauce over each. Repeat the layers, finishing with the chocolate sauce.

- Decorate with a few mini marshmallows and a little grated chocolate. Serve immediately with long spoons.

2 Rocky Road Cookies

Place 8 tablespoons (1 stick) softened unsalted butter and ½ cup packed light brown sugar in a bowl and beat with a handheld electric mixer until light and fluffy. Whisk in 1 beaten egg and 1 tablespoon milk. Fold in 1 tablespoon unsweetened cocoa powder, 1 cup all-purpose flour, ½ teaspoon baking powder, and 1 oz each of white and milk chocolate chunks. Place tablespoons of the mixture onto 2 baking sheets lined with parchment paper, spacing them well apart. Flatten slightly and place in a preheated oven, at 375°F, for 5 minutes or until the edges start to become firm. Remove from the oven and sprinkle with ½ cup miniature marshmallows and 1 oz each of white and dark chocolate chunks, pressing them into the cookies. Return to the oven for an additional 5–6 minutes until still slightly soft to the touch. Let cool on the baking sheet for 5 minutes, then transfer to a wire rack. Serve with scoops of vanilla ice cream. Store any leftover cookies in an airtight container.

3 Rocky Road Clusters

Melt 4 oz semisweet dark chocolate, broken into small pieces, 1 tablespoon light corn syrup, and 4 tablespoons unsalted butter in a small saucepan, stirring occasionally, until smooth and shiny. Stir in 1 cup chocolate chip cookie pieces and 1⅓ cups miniature marshmallows. Spoon into 12 cupcake liners and chill for 20 minutes until set. Serve with coffee. Store any leftover clusters in an airtight container for up to 3–4 days.

2 Sesame Banana Fritters with Peanut Butter Sauce

Serves 4

⅓ cup self-rising flour
2 tablespoons sesame seeds
1 egg, separated
⅓ cup cold milk
4 bananas, each cut into
   4 diagonal slices
vegetable oil, for frying

For the peanut butter sauce

½ cup smooth peanut butter
grated rind and juice of 1 lime
½ cup water

- To make the sauce, place the peanut butter, lime rind and juice, and measured water in a saucepan and cook over low heat, stirring, until smooth.

- Place the flour and sesame seeds in a bowl and make a well in the center. Add the egg yolk and milk and gradually whisk into the flour to form a thick batter. Whisk the egg white in a clean bowl with a handheld electric mixer until stiff, then fold into the batter. Tip the bananas into the batter and stir lightly to coat.

- Heat 2 inches of oil in a wok or large skillet until a drop of batter rises to the surface surrounded by bubbles and starts to brown. Add the bananas and fry for 3–4 minutes until crisp. Remove with a slotted spoon and drain on paper towels.

- Serve immediately with the peanut butter sauce.

---

1 **Pan-Fried Banana, Peanut Butter and Choc Sandwiches** Beat together 2 extra-large eggs and 1 cup milk in a shallow dish. Spread 2 tablespoons peanut butter on 1 slice of white bread and chocolate spread on another slice. Thinly slice 1 large banana and place half on top of the peanut butter, then sandwich the bread slices together. Press down lightly. Place in the egg mixture and let soak, then turn over. Repeat to make 1 more sandwich. Heat a little unsalted butter in a large skillet, add the sandwiches, and cook for 2–3 minutes on each side until golden brown. Cut in half diagonally and serve one half per person.

3 **Banana Bread and Peanut Butter Pudding** Remove the crusts from 8 medium slices of white bread. Spread the slices with ⅓ cup smooth peanut butter, then cut each slice in half. Thinly slice 3 bananas and place half in the bottom of a buttered 1 quart ovenproof dish. Arrange the bread over the top and add the remaining bananas. Pour over 1¾ cups prepared vanilla pudding and let stand for 5 minutes. Sprinkle with 2 tablespoons Demerara sugar, then place in a preheated oven, at 350°F, for 20 minutes, until bubbling.

Date, Maple Syrup, and Pecan Puddings

Serves 6

10 tablespoons (1¼ sticks)
  unsalted butter, diced, plus
  extra for greasing
1⅓ cups pitted dates
1 cup cold water
¼ cup maple syrup,
  plus 6 teaspoons
3 eggs, beaten
1⅓ cups self-rising flour
½ cup chopped pecans
freshly prepared custard
  (see page 150) or whipped
  cream, to serve

- Lightly grease six ⅔ cup metal molds or ramekins and place on a baking sheet. Place the dates and measured water in a small saucepan and bring to a boil, then cover and simmer gently for 5–6 minutes. Transfer to a large bowl and mash them with the back of a spoon or fork.

- Stir in the butter and the ¼ cup maple syrup and stir until the butter has melted, then gently stir in the eggs, flour, and pecans.

- Place 1 teaspoonful of maple syrup in each of the prepared molds and spoon in the sponge mixture. Place in a preheated oven, at 350°F, for 20 minutes or until risen and firm to the touch. Let cool in the molds for a few minutes.

- Turn out the puddings into bowls and serve with custard.

---

1 Date and Maple Syrup Sauce

Place 4 tablespoons unsalted butter, 2 tablespoons light brown sugar, 2 tablespoons maple syrup, and ⅔ cup chopped, pitted dates in a saucepan over low heat and stir until the butter has melted and the sugar has dissolved. Stir in 3 tablespoons heavy cream and simmer for 2–3 minutes until thickened. Serve poured over ice cream.

2 Date and Maple Syrup Pie

Place an 8 inch store-bought piecrust on a baking sheet. Cut 15 Medjool dates in half and remove the pits. Place 6 tablespoons unsalted butter, 3 tablespoons maple syrup, and ¼ cup packed light brown sugar in a saucepan and cook over low heat, stirring, until the sugar has dissolved. Stir in 1 cup walnut or pecan pieces and the dates. Spoon the mixture into the piecrust. Place the tart in a preheated oven, at 350°F, for 12–15 minutes. Let cool slightly before serving.

Sherry Trifle

Serves 6–8

6 shortcakes
½ cup sweet sherry (optional)
½ cup raspberry preserves or jam
1 tablespoon lemon juice
2 cups raspberries
1¾ cups whipping cream
¼ cup slivered almonds,
   toasted, to decorate

For the custard

2 cups milk
2 teaspoons vanilla extract
4 egg yolks
¼ cup superfine sugar
2 teaspoons cornstarch

- To make the custard, place the milk and vanilla extract in a saucepan and heat until just below boiling point. Place the egg yolks, sugar, and cornstarch in a heatproof bowl and beat with a handheld electric mixer until pale and thick, then gradually beat in the warm milk. Return to the pan and cook over medium heat for 2–3 minutes, beating continuously, until the custard has thickened. Transfer to a bowl, cover with plastic wrap to prevent a skin from forming, and chill.

- Meanwhile, arrange the shortcakes in the bottom of a deep, 8 inch bowl and pour over the sherry, if using. Mix together the preserves and lemon juice in a bowl and spoon over the cake. Add the raspberries and top with the cooled custard.

- Lightly whip the cream in a bowl with a handheld electric mixer until it forms soft peaks. Spoon on top of the custard and decorate with the almonds. Serve immediately or chill until ready to serve.

---

1 Quick Raspberry Trifles

Slice an 11½ oz store-bought pound cake into ½ inch thick pieces and sandwich together with ⅓ cup raspberry preserves or jam. Cut into cubes, then divide among 6 glasses. Pour over ½ cup sherry (optional) and top with 1⅔ cups raspberries. Spoon 1¾ cups store-bought vanilla pudding or freshly prepared custard over the top. Lightly whip 1¼ cups heavy cream in a bowl with a handheld electric mixer until it forms soft peaks, then spoon over the top. Decorate with extra raspberries and serve immediately.

2 Open Summer Trifle

Place 1¼ cups dessert wine (optional) and ⅓ cup superfine sugar in a saucepan and gently bring to a boil, then simmer for 7–8 minutes until syrupy. Cut 11½ oz store-bought pound cake into thick pieces and divide among 6 plates, then drizzle over half the syrup. Lightly whip 1¾ cups heavy cream in a bowl with a handheld electric mixer until it forms soft peaks, then spoon on top of the cakes. Top with 3 pitted and sliced peaches or nectarines and 1½ cups raspberries and

drizzle with the remaining syrup. Serve immediately.

 Key Lime Pie

Serves 6–8

2 cups crushed Graham crackers

7 tablespoons unsalted butter, melted

3 extra-large egg yolks

1 tablespoon grated lime rind

14 oz can sweetened condensed milk

juice of 4–5 limes, about ⅔ cup

To decorate

whipped cream

lime slices

- Stir the crushed crackers into the melted butter and press into the bottom and sides of a deep, 8 inch loose-bottom tart pan. Place on a baking sheet and bake in a preheated oven, at 350°F, for 5 minutes.

- Meanwhile, place the egg yolks and lime rind in a bowl and beat with a handheld electric mixer for 3–4 minutes until thickened. Pour in the condensed milk and continue whisking for an additional 5 minutes. Whisk in the the lime juice.

- Pour the mixture into the pan and return to the oven for an additional 8–10 minutes or until set. Let cool in the pan for 5 minutes, then chill for an additional 5 minutes.

- Serve the pie in slices, decorated with whipped cream and lime slices.

1 **Chocolate, Lime, and Mascarpone Creams** Stir 1¼ cups crushed plain chocolate cookies into 2 tablespoons melted unsalted butter and divide among 6 small glasses. Place 1 cup mascarpone cheese, the rind and juice of 2 limes, ⅔ cup heavy cream, and ⅓ cup confectioners' sugar in a large bowl and beat together with a handheld electric mixer until thick. Spoon over the cookies, top with a little grated chocolate, and serve.

 2 **No-Bake Key Lime Pie** Stir 2 cups crushed Graham crackers into 6 tablespoons melted unsalted butter and press into the sides and bottom of a deep, 8 inch loose-bottom tart pan. Place 1¼ cups heavy cream, the juice and grated rind of 4 limes, and ¾ cup canned sweetened condensed milk in a large bowl and beat together with a handheld electric mixer until thick and creamy. Spoon over the bottom and chill until ready to serve.

30 Creamy Lemon and Almond Rice Pudding

Serves 4

½ cup short-grain rice, rinsed
¼ cup superfine sugar
grated rind and juice of
   2 unwaxed lemons, plus
   extra rind to decorate
⅔ cup golden raisins
2 cup boiling water
12 oz can evaporated milk
¼ cup slivered almonds

- Place the rice, sugar, lemon rind and juice, golden raisins, and measured water in a saucepan and simmer, uncovered, for 20–25 minutes. Stir in the evaporated milk and simmer for an additional 5 minutes until the rice is tender.

- Meanwhile, place the almonds in a hot skillet and dry-fry for 1–2 minutes until toasted.

- Pour the rice pudding into warmed serving dishes and sprinkle with the slivered almonds and extra lemon rind. Serve immediately.

1 ◐ Fast Lemon Rice Pudding

Place 3½ cups store-bought rice pudding in a saucepan and heat gently for a few minutes until heated through. Stir in the grated rind and juice of 2 lemons and ⅔ cup golden raisins. Serve sprinkled with ¼ cup toasted almonds.

2 ◐ Fruity Cranberry and Golden Raisin

Risotto Place ¾ cup risotto rice, 4¼ cups milk, ⅓ cup golden raisins, 2 tablespoons superfine sugar, ⅓ cup dried cranberries, and 1 teaspoon vanilla extract in a large saucepan and bring to a boil. Reduce the heat and simmer, uncovered, for 15–20 minutes, stirring occasionally, until the rice is tender. Serve immediately.

Ginger Cakes with Caramel Sauce

Serves 4

4 tablespoons unsalted butter
⅔ cup light brown sugar
2 tablespoons light corn syrup
1 teaspoon vanilla extract
⅔ cup heavy cream
11 oz store-bought ginger cake, cut into 8 thick slices
vanilla ice cream, to serve (optional)

- Place the butter, sugar, and light corn syrup in a saucepan over low heat and cook, stirring, until the sugar has dissolved. Bring to a boil, then gently bubble for 2–3 minutes. Add the vanilla extract and cream and stir well. Let cool slightly.

- Place 2 slices of the ginger cake in the bottom of four 1 cup ovenproof dishes, then pour the caramel sauce over the top. Place on a baking sheet and bake in a preheated oven, at 350°F, for 12–15 minutes or until bubbling.

- Let stand for 4–5 minutes, then serve with scoops of vanilla ice cream, if using.

---

1 Caramel and Ginger Sauce

Place 1¼ cups heavy cream and ½ cup packed dark brown sugar in a saucepan and heat gently until the sugar has dissolved. Stir in 1 finely chopped piece of preserved ginger in syrup and 2 tablespoons preserved ginger syrup (taken from the jar) and bring to a boil, then cook for 2–3 minutes until thickened. Serve poured over ice cream.

2 Quick Ginger Cake with Caramel

Sauce Thickly slice an 11 oz store-bought ginger cake and place in a 1-quart ovenproof dish. Pour over 1 cup store-bought dulche de leche (thick caramel). Place in a preheated oven, at 350°F, for 15 minutes or until bubbling. Let stand for 2–3 minutes before serving with vanilla ice cream.

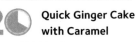

Mini Shoofly pies

Serves 6–8

1½ cups light corn syrup
2 cupsfresh white bread crumbs
grated rind of 1 large lemon
1 egg, beaten
8 single-serving,
  store-bought piecrusts
vanilla ice cream or heavy cream,
  to serve

- Place the light corn syrup in a saucepan and heat gently until thinned in consistency. Remove from the heat and stir in the bread crumbs, lemon rind, and beaten egg. Transfer the mixture to a pitcher.

- Place the piecrusts on a baking sheet, then divide the filling evenly among them. Place in a preheated oven, at 350°F, for 12–15 minutes or until lightly set and golden.

- Let cool slightly, then serve warm with ice cream or cream.

1 Banana Waffles with Pecan Syrup

Place ½ cup light corn syrup and ½ cup chopped pecans in a small saucepan and heat gently until warmed through. Lightly toast 6 waffles and place in 6 bowls. Slice 6 bananas and arrange over the top of the waffles, then place a scoop of vanilla ice cream on each. Drizzle the warm pecan syrup over and serve immediately.

3 Orange-Flavored Shoofly Pie

Place an 8 inch store-bought piecrust on a baking sheet. Place 1¼ cups light corn syrup in a saucepan and heat gently until thinned in consistency. Remove from the heat and stir in 2 cups fresh white bread crumbs, the grated rind of 1 orange, and 1 beaten egg. Pour into the piecrust and bake in a preheated oven, at 350°F, for 15–20 minutes or until set. Serve warm.

3⟨ Blueberry and Lemon Sponge Puddings

Serves 4

7 tablespoons unsalted
  butter, softened, plus
  extra for greasing
1 lemon
4 teaspoons light corn syrup
½ cup superfine sugar
2 extra-large eggs
¾ cup self-rising flour, sifted
1 cup blueberries
custard (see page 150) or light
  cream, to serve (optional)

- Lightly grease four 1 cup metal molds or ramekins and line the bottoms with nonstick parchment paper. Place on a baking sheet. Grate the rind from the lemon and cut in half. Cut 4 thin slices from 1 half, reserving the remaining half.

- Place a lemon slice in the bottom of each prepared mold, then drizzle 1 teaspoon of the light corn syrup over each.

- Place the butter, sugar, and grated lemon rind in a large bowl and beat with a handheld electric mixer until light and fluffy. Beat in the eggs, then squeeze over the juice of the remaining lemon half. Fold in the flour and blueberries.

- Spoon the mixture into the molds and spread the tops level. Place in a preheated oven, at 375°F, for 15–20 minutes or until risen and firm to the touch. Let cool in the molds for a few minutes. Turn out the puddings onto plates and serve with cream or custard, if using.

1⟨ Blueberry Sponges with Lemon Cream

Coarsely chop 2 blueberry muffins and divide among 4 bowls. Place 1¾ cups blueberries, ¼ cup superfine sugar, and 2 tablespoons lemon juice in a saucepan and cook over low heat, stirring, until the sugar has dissolved and the berries start to burst, then spoon the berries and juice over the sponges. Place 1 cup crème fraîche, 1 cup Greek yogurt, 1 tablespoon confectioners' sugar, 2 teaspoons grated lemon rind, and 1 tablespoon lemon juice in a bowl and beat together. Spoon over the blueberries and serve immediately.

2⟨ Lemon–Blueberry Coulis with Meringues

Place 1 cup blueberries, 1 tablespoon superfine sugar, and the juice of 1 lemon in a saucepan and bring to a boil. Reduce the heat and simmer for 5 minutes until the berries start to break down. Press through a strainer into a bowl to make a coulis, then let cool. Whip ⅔ cup heavy cream in a bowl with a handheld electric mixer until just beginning to thicken, then fold in 1¼ cups Greek yogurt, 3 tablespoons lemon curd, 2 crushed meringue nests, and ⅔ cup blueberries. Spoon one-third of the cream mixture into a large serving dish. Drizzle with a tablespoon of the coulis. Repeat this twice, then finish with a layer of the cream and a drizzle of coulis. Serve immediately.

 Apple Tart

Serves 6–8

12 oz package chilled puff pastry
flour, for dusting
5 apples, cored and cut
  into thin slices
juice of 1 lemon
4 tablespoons unsalted
  butter, diced
3 tablespoons superfine sugar
¼ cup apricot preserves
vanilla ice cream, to serve
  (optional)

- Line a large baking sheet with nonstick parchment paper. Roll out the pastry onto a lightly floured surface to a 14 inch square, trimming the edges if necessary, to make a neat square. Place on the baking sheet and scrunch up the edges of the pastry to prevent the filling from running out.

- Toss the apples in the lemon juice. Dot some of the butter over the bottom of the pastry and sprinkle with 1 tablespoon of the sugar.

- Arrange the apples in neat rows on the pastry, then dot with the remaining butter and sprinkle over the remaining sugar.

- Place in a preheated oven, at 425°F, for 15–20 minutes or until golden and crisp.

- Warm the apricot preserves in a small saucepan, then brush over the apples and pastry. Serve immediately with scoops of vanilla ice cream, if using.

Speedy Apple Compote

Melt 4 tablespoons unsalted butter in a saucepan, then add 4 peeled, cored, and chopped apples, 2 tablespoons superfine sugar, and ½ teaspoon ground cinnamon. Cook for about 5 minutes, stirring occasionally, until the apples have softened. Serve with vanilla yogurt.

Individual Apple Tarts

Unroll a 12 oz package chilled rolled puff pastry and cut out six 6½ x 3½ inch rectangles, then place on a baking sheet. Using a sharp knife, score a ½ inch border around the edge, but do not cut all the way through. Prick the center of each bottom with a fork. Divide 1 tablespoon diced unsalted butter over the bottoms and sprinkle with 1 tablespoon superfine sugar. Arrange 4 cored and sliced apples among the pastries, dot with another 1 tablespoon diced butter, and scatter over another tablespoon of superfine sugar. Bake in a preheated oven, at 400°F, for 12–15 minutes or until risen and golden. Brush 2 tablespoons warmed apricot preserves over the top of each and serve immediately.

Baked New York Cheesecakes

Serves 6

²/₃ cup crushed Graham crackers
2 tablespoons unsalted butter, melted
1 cup light cream cheese
¼ cup superfine sugar
¼ cup sour cream
finely grated rind of ½ lemon
1 teaspoon vanilla extract
1 tablespoon cornstarch
2 eggs
raspberries, to serve
confectioners' sugar, for dusting

- Line a 6-hole muffin pan with paper liners. Stir the crushed crackers into the melted butter and press into the bottom of the liners. Chill while you make the filling.

- Place the cream cheese, sugar, sour cream, lemon rind, vanilla extract, cornstarch, and eggs in a bowl and beat together.

- Spoon the mixture over the cookie base and place in a preheated oven, at 325°F, for 20 minutes. Let cool in the pan for 5 minutes.

- Remove the cheesecakes from the liners and place on a serving plate. Serve warm decorated with raspberries and a dusting of confectioners' sugar.

1 Instant New York Cheesecakes

Place 1 cup cream cheese, 2 tablespoons confectioners' sugar, ½ cup sour cream, ½ teaspoon vanilla extract, and 1 tablespoon grated lemon rind in a bowl and beat together. Spoon the mixture onto 12 Graham crackers and decorate each with 2 raspberries. Serve 2 cheesecakes per person.

2 New York Cheesecake

in a Glass Crush 7 Graham crackers and divide among 6 glasses. Place 1½ cups cream cheese, 1 cup sour cream, 2 tablespoons confectioners' sugar, 1 teaspoon vanilla extract, and the grated rind of ½ lemon in a bowl and beat together. Spoon into the glasses, top with a few raspberries, and chill for 10 minutes before serving.

DES-FAMI-NAS

 # Chocolate and Apricot Crunch

Serves 4

8 oz orange-flavored semisweet dark chocolate (70 percent cocoa solids)

8 tablespoons (1 stick) unsalted butter

1 tablespoon light corn syrup

4 meringue nests, broken into small pieces

1 cup chocolate chip cookie pieces

1 cup dried apricots, chopped

unsweetened cocoa powder, for dusting

- Line a 7 x 11 inch rectangular cake pan with nonstick parchment paper. Place the chocolate, butter, and light corn syrup in a small saucepan and heat gently, stirring occasionally, until smooth and shiny.

- Place all remaining ingredients in a large bowl and mix well, then pour over the chocolate mixture. Stir until all the ingredients are evenly coated.

- Tip the mixture into the prepared pan and even it out with the back of a spoon. Place in the freezer for 10 minutes, then chill in the refrigerator for an additional 10 minutes until firm.

- Run a knife around the edge of the pan, turn out onto a board and remove the parchment paper. Dust the surface with cocoa powder and cut into 16 slices. Store any leftover bars in an airtight container for up to 3–4 days.

Chocolate and Apricot Crunch

Layer Mix together 2 cups Greek yogurt and ¼ cup confectioners' sugar, sifted, in a bowl. Spoon half the mixture into 4 glasses, then top each with 2 canned apricot halves. Divide ½ cup chocolate granola between the glasses, then spoon the remaining yogurt over the top. Serve immediately.

 ## Nutty Chocolate Crunch

Place 4 oz milk chocolate, 2 tablespoons light corn syrup, and 2 tablespoons unsalted butter in a saucepan and heat gently, stirring, until melted, then stir in 1 cup granola with nuts. Tip the mixture onto a baking sheet lined with nonstick parchment paper and chill for 10–15 minutes. To serve, coarsely break up the granola and spoon over ice cream.

Lemon Meringue Pie

Serves 6

8 inch store-bought piecrust
14 oz can light condensed milk
2 eggs yolks
grated rind and juice of 2 lemons

For the meringue

4 egg whites
1 cup superfine sugar

- Place the piecrust on a baking sheet. Place the condensed milk, egg yolks, and lemon rind and juice in a large bowl and beat together. Pour into the piecrust to ½ inch below the top.

- Whisk the egg whites in a clean large bowl with a handheld electric mixer until they form soft peaks, then gradually whisk in the sugar until the mixture is thick and glossy.

- Pile the meringue on top of the lemon mixture and place in a preheated oven, at 375°F, for 15–20 minutes until golden and crisp.

---

1 **Lemon Meringue Kisses**

Lightly whip 1¼ cups heavy cream in a bowl with a handheld electric mixer until it forms soft peaks, then stir in 2–3 tablespoons lemon curd. Sandwich together 24 mini meringue shells with the lemon cream. Serve 2 meringues per person, dusted with confectioners' sugar.

2 **Meringue and Lemon Curd**

Coarsely crush 8 meringue nests into different sizes. Lightly whip 1¼ cups heavy cream in a large bowl with a handheld electric mixer until it forms soft peaks, then stir in 2–3 tablespoons lemon curd to taste and ⅔ cup Greek yogurt. Gently stir in the crushed meringues, then spoon into 6 glasses. Drizzle the tops with a little extra lemon curd. Chill for 10 minutes before serving.

30 Mincemeat and Apple Strudel

Serves 6

2 small apples, peeled, cored, and diced

¾ cup mincemeat

½ cup chopped pecans

4 sheets of phyllo pastry, about 19 x 10 inches

4 tablespoons unsalted butter, melted

confectioners' sugar, for dusting

vanilla ice cream, to serve (optional)

- Mix together the apples, mincemeat, and pecans in a bowl.

- Lay the first sheet of phyllo pastry on a clean dish towel on a flat surface and brush with melted butter. Repeat with the remaining sheets of pastry.

- Spread the mincemeat mixture over the pastry, leaving a 1 inch border. Fold in the ends over the filling, then roll up like a jelly roll, from one long edge, using the dish towel. Once rolled up, press the strudel gently together. Place on a baking sheet and brush with the remaining butter.

- Place in a preheated oven, at 350°F, for about 20 minutes or until golden brown. Dust with confectioners' sugar and serve with scoops of vanilla ice cream, if using.

---

1 Mincemeat Bundles

Fold 12 sheets of phyllo pastry, 19 x 10 inches, in half and brush with melted unsalted butter. Place 1 tablespoon mincemeat in the center of each square, then draw up the edges and scrunch together. Place on a baking sheet and brush with melted butter. Place in a preheated oven, at 375°F, for 6–8 minutes or until golden. Serve 2 bundles per person, dusted with confectioners' sugar.

2 Mini Mincemeat and Apple Pies

Unroll a 12 oz package chilled, rolled puff pastry and cut out twelve 4 inch circles. Place the circles on a baking sheet. Using a 3½ inch cutter, press into the center of each circle to make an indent, but do not cut all the way through. Brush the edge of each circle with a little milk. Mix together 1⅓ cups mincemeat, 1 peeled, cored, and diced apple, and 3 tablespoons dried cranberries in a bowl. Spoon 1 tablespoon of mincemeat mixture into the center of each circle, then sprinkle over ½ cup chopped pecans. Place on the top shelf of a preheated oven, at 425°F, for 12–15 minutes or until golden. Serve 2 warm pies per person, dusted with confectioners' sugar.

10 Caramel Dipping Sauce with Fresh Fruit

Serves 4–6

6 tablespoons unsalted butter
¾ cup light brown sugar
2 tablespoons light corn syrup
1 teaspoon vanilla extract
⅔ cup heavy cream
apple wedges and bananas
   chunks, for dipping

- Place the butter, sugar, light corn syrup, and vanilla extract in a heavy nonstick saucepan and stir over low heat until the butter has melted and the sugar has dissolved. Add the cream, stirring continuously. Bring back to a boil and simmer for 5 minutes until thickened.

- Pour into a bowl and let stand for a few minutes before serving with the apples and bananas, for dipping.

2 Hazelnut and Caramel Sauce

Place ½ cup chopped hazelnuts in a skillet and dry-fry over medium heat for 2–3 minutes, stirring occasionally, until toasted. Place ⅓ cup superfine sugar and ⅓ cup water in a small heavy saucepan and heat gently until the sugar has dissolved. Bring to a boil and boil rapidly until the caramel is a deep golden color. Immerse the bottom of the pan in cold water to prevent the caramel from becoming too dark. Carefully add 2 tablespoons water, then stir in the hazelnuts and 4 tablespoons unsalted butter until the sauce is smooth and glossy. Serve immediately poured over ice cream.

3 Hazelnut Caramel Brittle

Line a baking sheet with a lightly oiled piece of aluminum foil. Melt ½ cup superfine sugar in a heavy saucepan over low heat. Do not stir the sugar, but gently shake the pan from time to time to redistribute the sugar and prevent it from overcooking in one place. When all the sugar has melted and turned a rich golden caramel color, quickly stir in 1 cup coarsely chopped toasted hazelnuts. Pour out immediately onto the oiled foil and let cool and harden. When set, place in a strong food bag and bash with a rolling pin. Serve sprinkled over ice cream or chocolate mousse.

Quick Rosewater and Cardamom Rice Pudding

Serves 4–6

3½ cups prepared rice pudding
2 teaspoons rosewater
6 cardamom pods, crushed
½ cup pistachio nuts, chopped

- Place the rice pudding in a saucepan, stir in the rosewater and cardamom pods, and heat gently for 5–6 minutes until heated through. Stir in ¼ cup of the pistachios.

- Serve in bowls decorated with the remaining pistachios.

2 **Rosewater and Cardamom Rice Pudding with Poached Figs**

Place ½ cup sugar, 1¼ cups water, and 2 teaspoons rosewater in a saucepan and stir over medium heat until the sugar has dissolved, then bring to a boil and cook for 5 minutes. Reduce the heat and add 8 halved figs. Cook gently for 8–10 minutes until tender. Meanwhile, make the rice pudding as above. Serve with the poached figs and their syrup and sprinkled with the pistachios.

3 **Homemade Spiced Rice Pudding**

Place ½ cup rinsed short-grain rice, ¼ cup superfine sugar, 2 teaspoons rosewater, 6 crushed cardamom pods, and 2 cups boiling water in a saucepan and simmer, uncovered, for 20–25 minutes. Stir in a 12 oz can evaporated milk and simmer for an additional 5 minutes. Spoon into 4 bowls and serve decorated with chopped pistachios.

Chocolate Fondue with Hazelnut Straws

Serves 6

8 oz semisweet dark chocolate
(75 percent cocoa solids),
broken into pieces

1¼ cups heavy cream

2 tablespoons unsalted butter

2 tablespoons brandy or orange
liqueur (optional)

For the phyllo straws

3 sheets of phyllo pastry,
about 10 x 9 inches

2 tablespoons unsalted
butter, melted

2 tablespoons superfine sugar

½ cup chopped hazelnuts

- To make the phyllo straws, line a baking sheet with nonstick parchment paper. Place 1 sheet of phyllo pastry on the baking sheet, brush with one-third of the melted butter, and sprinkle over one-third of the sugar and hazelnuts. Continue with the remaining ingredients, finishing with the hazelnuts and sugar on top.

- Cut the pastry in half lengthwise, then cut into 28 strips, about ½ inch wide and separate slightly. Place in a preheated oven, at 350°F, for 4–5 minutes or until golden. Let cool on a wire rack while you make the fondue.

- Place the chocolate, cream, butter, and brandy or orange liqueur, if using, in a heatproof bowl set over a saucepan of gently simmering water. Heat gently for 5–7 minutes, stirring occasionally, until the mixture is smooth and glossy.

- Pour into a fondue pot or warm bowl and serve immediately with the hazelnut straws, for dipping.

Hazelnut Straws with Ice cream and Chocolate Sauce

Make the hazelnut straws as above. Meanwhile, place 1¼ cups store-bought chocolate sauce and 1 tablespoon orange liqueur (optional) in a small saucepan and heat gently to warm through. Dip 6 individual containers of vanilla ice cream in hot water and turn out. Drizzle with the chocolate sauce and serve with the warm hazelnut straws.

Chocolate Fondue with Puff Pastry Hazelnut Straws

Process ⅔ cup hazelnuts in a food processor until finely chopped, then add 1 teaspoon ground cinnamon and 1 tablespoon superfine sugar and process together. Sprinkle some of the mixture on a clean surface and unroll a 12 oz pack chilled, rolled puff pastry on top. Sprinkle over half the nut mixture, press into the pastry, then roll out to a 12 x 9 inch rectangle. Sprinkle over the remaining nut mixture and gently roll it in. Cut widthwise into ½ inch wide strips and then twist them. Place on a large baking sheet and bake in a preheated oven, at 400°F, for 15–20 minutes or until golden. Meanwhile, make the fondue as above and serve with the warm straws.

QuickCook
Entertaining

Recipes listed by cooking time

3O

2O

 Tiramisu

Serves 4–6

1 cup mascarpone cheese
1 cup store-bought vanilla
   pudding or freshly prepared
   vanilla custard (see page 150)
3 tablespoons Marsala or brandy
⅔ cup cold strong black coffee
16–18 ladyfingers
2 tablespoons unsweetened
   cocoa powder

- Place the mascarpone, vanilla pudding, Marsala, and
  1 tablespoon of the coffee in a large bowl and beat with
  a handheld electric mixer for 2–3 minutes until light,
  fluffy, and smooth.

- Take one ladyfinger at a time and dip into the cold coffee,
  being careful not to let the sponge get too soggy. Line a
  shallow dish with half the ladyfingers or divide among
  shallow individual dishes. Spoon over half the creamy
  mixture, then sift over half the cocoa powder.

- Repeat with the remaining coffee-dipped ladyfingers,
  creamy mixture, and cocoa powder. Chill until ready
  to serve.

---

1 **Tiramisu Affogato**
Place 1 cup heavy
whipping cream, 1 tablespoon
confectioners' sugar, and
1 tablespoon Marsala (optional)
in a bowl and beat with a
handheld electric mixer until it
forms soft peaks. Place 1 scoop
of vanilla ice cream and 1 scoop
of coffee ice cream in each of
4 heatproof glasses or cups.
Top each with 1 Italian Savoiardi
(ladyfinger) cookie. Pour a shot
of hot espresso over each and
spoon on the lightly whipped
cream. Dust with unsweetened
cocoa powder and serve.

3 **Strawberry and
White Chocolate
Tiramisu** Melt 5 oz white
chocolate, broken into small
pieces, in a heatproof bowl set
over a saucepan of gently
simmering water. Place 1 cup
mascarpone cheese and 1 cup
store-bought vanilla pudding
or freshly prepared custard
(see page 150) in a bowl and
beat in the melted chocolate.
Dip 16 ladyfingers in 1 cup
sweet dessert wine and place
half in the bottom of a shallow
dish. Cover with 2 cups hulled
and sliced strawberries,

reserving a few for decoration,
then spoon over half the
chocolate mixture. Repeat the
ladyfinger and chocolate layers.
Chill for 10 minutes, then serve
decorated with the reserved
strawberries.

 Affogato al Caffe

Serves 4

8 balls of good-quality vanilla
  ice cream
4 freshly made espresso coffees
8 amaretti cookies, to serve

- Scoop 2 balls of the ice cream into each of 4 cappuccino cups or latte glasses. Pour a cup of hot coffee quickly over each.

- Serve immediately, with the cookies for dunking.

2 Affogato al Caffe with Vanilla Syrup

Place 1 cup superfine sugar, 1 cup water, and 1 vanilla bean, split lengthwise and seeds scraped out, in a saucepan. Stir over low heat until the sugar has dissolved, then increase the heat and simmer for 6 minutes. Scoop the ice cream into 4 heatproof cups or glasses as above. Remove the vanilla bean from the pan and spoon 1 tablespoon of the syrup over each ice cream before pouring over the hot coffee as above. The remaining syrup can be poured over fruit.

3 Affogato al Caffe with Almond

Macaroons Mix together ½ cup ground almonds and ⅓ cup superfine sugar in a bowl. Beat 1 extra-large egg white and ¼ teaspoon almond extract in a clean bowl with a handheld electric mixer until stiff, then fold in the ground almond mixture. Place teaspoons of the mixture, slightly apart, on 2 large baking sheets lined with nonstick parchment paper. Place in preheated oven, at 350°F, for 15 minutes. Cool on the baking sheets for 5 minutes, then place on a wire rack. Make the above recipe and serve with the macaroons for dunking.

30 Lemon and Lime Puddings with Sauce

Serves 4

4 tablespoons unsalted butter, softened

⅔ cup superfine sugar

grated rind and juice of 1 small lemon

grated rind and juice of 1 lime

2 extra-large eggs, separated

⅓ cup plus 1 tablespoon self-rising flour

1¼ cups milk

- Place the butter, sugar, and lemon and lime rind in a large bowl and beat with a handheld electric mixer until light and fluffy. Add the egg yolks and flour and beat in (the mixture will look curdled), then beat in the lemon and lime juice and milk.

- Beat the egg whites in a clean bowl with a handheld electric mixer until stiff, then gently fold into the lemon and lime mixture.

- Put four 1 cup ovenproof dishes in a roasting pan and pour the pudding mixture into the dishes. Pour enough water into the pan to come halfway up the sides of the dishes.

- Place in a preheated oven, at 350°F, for 20 minutes or until the tops are golden brown and spongy and there is a lemon and lime sauce in the bottom. Serve immediately.

1 Lime Curd Tarts

Melt 6 tablespoons unsalted butter in a heavy saucepan, then add 3 extra-large eggs, ⅓ cup superfine sugar, ½ cup lime juice, and the grated rind of 1 lime. Cook over low heat, beating continuously, until it has thickened and formed a custard. Spoon into 4 single-serving, store-bought piecrusts and serve warm.

2 Lemon and Lime Syllabubs

Place ¼ cup superfine sugar, the juice of ½ lemon and 1 lime, and 1 teaspoon each finely grated lemon and lime rind in a bowl and stir to dissolve the sugar. Lightly whip 1 cup heavy cream in a bowl with a handheld electric mixer until it forms soft peaks, then slowly beat in ½ cup sweet white wine. Beat in the sugar mixture until the cream is thick and fluffy. Spoon into 4 glasses and decorate with a little lemon and lime rind. Serve immediately or chill until ready to serve.

 # Tangy Lemon Tarts

Serves 8

8 single-serving,
   store-bought piecrusts
¼ cup granulated sugar
½ cup water
1 unwaxed lemon, cut into
   8 thin slices

For the lemon filling

2 extra-large eggs
⅓ cup superfine sugar
finely grated rind and juice
   of 2 unwaxed lemons
½ cup heavy cream

- To make the lemon filling, place all the ingredients in a food processor or blender and blend until smooth. Transfer to a pitcher.

- Place the piecrusts on a baking sheet and pour in the lemon filling. Place in the center of a preheated oven, at 300°F, for about 15 minutes or until just set. Let cool slightly.

- Meanwhile, place the granulated sugar and measured water in a saucepan and heat gently, stirring occasionally, until the sugar has completely dissolved. Add the lemon slices and simmer, uncovered, for 12–15 minutes. Transfer to a piece of nonstick parchment paper to cool slightly.

- Serve the warm tarts topped with the lemon slices.

 Instant Lemon Tarts

Place 1 cup mascarpone cheese and ⅓–½ cup lemon curd, to taste, in a bowl and beat together. Spoon into 8 single-serving, store-bought piecrusts and serve, dusted with confectioners' sugar.

No-Cook Lemon Tart

Stir 2 cups crushed Graham crackers into 6 tablespoons melted unsalted butter and press into the sides and bottom of a deep, 8 inch loose-bottom tart pan. Chill while you make the filling. Place 1¼ cups heavy cream, the juice and grated rind of 2 lemons, ¾ cup canned sweetened condensed milk, and 2 tablespoons lemon curd in a large bowl and beat together with a handheld electric mixer until thick and creamy. Spoon over the cookie base. Chill for 10 minutes before serving.

 # White Chocolate and Raspberry Meringue Roulade

Serves 6

1 cup raspberries
1 oz white chocolate, melted,
   to serve

For the meringue

5 egg whites
1 cup superfine sugar
½ teaspoon white wine vinegar
1 teaspoon cornstarch
½ teaspoon vanilla extract

For the chocolate filling

5 oz white chocolate, broken into
   small pieces
⅔ cup crème fraîche

- To make the chocolate filling, melt the chocolate in a heatproof bowl set over a saucepan of gently simmering water, then let cool slightly. Place the crème fraîche in a bowl and stir in the melted chocolate. Chill while you make the meringue.

- Line an 8 x 12 inch jelly roll pan with nonstick parchment paper. Beat the egg whites in a clean large bowl with a handheld electric mixer until stiff, then gradually beat in the sugar until the mixture is thick and glossy. Gently fold in the vinegar, cornstarch, and vanilla extract.

- Spread the mixture into the prepared pan and place in the center of a preheated oven, at 350°F, for 15 minutes. Let cool in the pan for 5 minutes.

- Turn out the meringue onto another piece of parchment paper and spread the chocolate filling evenly over the top. Sprinkle with the raspberries and roll up the meringue.

- Transfer to a serving plate and drizzle with the melted white chocolate before serving.

 1 **Raspberry and White Chocolate Mini Pavlovas** Melt 5 oz white chocolate, broken into small pieces, in a heatproof bowl set over a saucepan of gently simmering water, then let cool slightly. Place ⅔ cup crème fraîche in a bowl and stir in the melted chocolate. Fill 6 meringue nests with the chocolate mixture, then top with 1 cup raspberries. Decorate with a little grated white chocolate. Serve immediately or chill until ready to serve.

2 **White Chocolate and Raspberry Meringue Creams** Melt 6 oz white chocolate, broken into small pieces, in a heatproof bowl set over a saucepan of gently simmering water. Cool slightly, then stir in ⅔ cup crème fraîche. Coarsely break up 6 meringue nests and divide them among 6 glasses. Divide 1⅓ cups raspberries among the glasses, reserving a few for decoration, then spoon over the chocolate mixture. Top with the reserved raspberries and a little grated white chocolate. Chill until ready to serve.

Salted Caramel Shards

Serves 4
½ cup superfine sugar
1 teaspoon coarse sea salt
chocolate ice cream, to serve

- Line a baking sheet with nonstick parchment paper. Place the sugar in a small, heavy saucepan over low heat. Do not stir. Watch the sugar until the bottom layer has melted, then reduce the heat and stir until the sugar has dissolved and is a light caramel color.

- Pour onto the baking sheet, sprinkle with the sea salt, and let harden.

- When set, after about 10 minutes, use a rolling pin to break into shards.

- Serve with chocolate ice cream or as a decoration for fools or syllabubs.

Salted Caramel Sauce

Place 8 tablespoons (1 stick) unsalted butter, ⅓ cup packed light brown sugar, ⅓ cup light corn syrup, 1 teaspoon vanilla extract, and 1 teaspoon coarse sea salt in a saucepan and melt over medium heat. Pour in 1¼ cups heavy cream and boil for 5 minutes until thickened slightly. Serve poured over ice cream.

Chocolate Salted Caramel Medallions

Make the caramel shards as above. Melt 4 oz semisweet dark chocolate, broken into small pieces, in a heatproof bowl set over a saucepan of gently simmering water. Meanwhile, draw circles about 1¾ inches in diameter onto a large sheet of nonstick parchment paper, turn the paper over, and use the lines as a guide. Spoon about ½ teaspoon of the melted chocolate inside each circle. Sprinkle over some salted caramel shards and let set. Serve as an accompaniment to ice cream.

Irish Coffee Syllabubs

Serves 4

½ cup superfine sugar
¼ cup cold, strong black coffee
¼ cup coffee liqueur
1¼ cups heavy cream
unsweetened cocoa powder,
 for dusting

For the topping

⅔ cup whipping cream
2 teaspoons vanilla sugar
2 tablespoons Irish whiskey
 (optional)
¼ cup ice-cold water

- Place the superfine sugar, coffee, liqueur, and heavy cream in a large bowl and beat with a handheld electric mixer until thickened and the beaters leave a trail when lifted above the mixture. Pour into 4 tall glasses and chill while you make the topping.

- To make the topping, place the whipping cream, vanilla sugar, whiskey, if using, and measured water in a bowl and beat with a handheld electric mixer until thick and frothy.

- Spoon the cappuccino topping over the syllabubs and dust with cocoa powder. Serve immediately or chill until ready to serve.

Irish Coffee Ice Creams

Place 2 scoops of vanilla ice cream in 4 heatproof glasses or cups, then add a shot of Irish whiskey to each. Pour 1 cup freshly made, strong black coffee over each and serve immediately.

Irish Coffee Creams

Dissolve 2 teaspoons espresso coffee powder in 2 tablespoons boiling water. Place 1 cup mascarpone cheese and 2 tablespoons confectioners' sugar in a heatproof bowl and beat in the coffee mixture with a handheld electric mixer until smooth. Beat in 1 cup heavy cream and 2 tablespoons Irish whiskey until creamy. Spoon into 4 glasses and chill for 10 minutes before serving.

DES-ENTE-PEJ

 Pan-Fried Figs with Marsala

Serves 4

4 tablespoons unsalted butter
8 large ripe figs, halved
2 tablespoons light brown sugar
⅓ cup Marsala
crème fraîche or mascarpone
  cheese, to serve

- Melt the butter in a nonstick skillet and place the figs into the frothing butter, cut side down. Cook for about 2 minutes until golden, then turn over.

- Sprinkle the sugar over the figs and cook for 2 minutes. Pour in the Marsala and let it bubble up, then reduce the heat and simmer for an additional 2–3 minutes to reduce the alcohol and produce a syrupy sauce.

- Spoon into bowls and serve immediately with dollops of crème fraîche or mascarpone cheese.

---

2 Figs with Marsala Sabayon

Grease four 1 cup ovenproof dishes or ramekins and place on a baking sheet. Stand 2 halves of a large fig in each. Place 5 egg yolks, 2 tablespoons superfine sugar, 2 tablespoons honey, and ⅓ cup Marsala in a heatproof bowl set over a saucepan of simmering water and beat with a handheld electric mixer for about 8 minutes until the mixture is thick and the beaters leave a trail when lifted above the mixture. Remove from the heat and continue to beat for an additional 4 minutes until cooled. Spoon the mixture over the figs and cook under a preheated hot broiler for 2–3 minutes or until golden. Serve immediately.

3 Roasted Figs with Honey and Marsala

Cut a deep cross into 8 figs and place in an ovenproof dish that has a lid. Drizzle over 2 tablespoons honey and ¼ cup Marsala. Cover with the lid and place in a preheated oven, at 400°F, for about 20 minutes. Serve with the juices and dollops of mascarpone cheese.

2  Vanilla Poached Pears with Warm Fudge Sauce

Serves 4

¼ cup superfine sugar
1 vanilla bean, split lengthwise
   and seeds scraped out
1 tablespoon lemon juice
2½ cups cold water
4 ripe pears, peeled, halved,
   and cored
vanilla ice cream, to serve
   (optional)

For the fudge sauce

6 tablespoons unsalted butter
⅔ cup packed light brown sugar
5 oz can evaporated milk
1 tablespoon light corn syrup

- Place the superfine sugar, vanilla bean and seeds, lemon juice, and measured water in a large saucepan and bring gradually to a boil, stirring occasionally, until the sugar has dissolved. Add the pears and simmer gently for 10–15 minutes or until tender.

- Meanwhile, place all the fudge sauce ingredients in a saucepan and cook gently over low heat for 2–3 minutes or until the butter has melted. Gently bring to a boil, stirring continuously, for 3–4 minutes until the sauce has thickened slightly. Remove from the heat and keep warm.

- Drain the pears from the syrup, divide among 4 serving plates, and pour the fudge sauce over the top. Serve immediately with vanilla ice cream, if using.

---

1 Pear and Fudge Sauce Ice Cream Sundaes Make the fudge sauce as above. Peel, core, and chop 4 ripe pears and divide among 4 sundae glasses. Add 1 large scoop of vanilla ice cream to each glass, then crumble 1 florentine cookie over each sundae. Top with the warm fudge sauce and serve immediately.

3 Baked Fudgy Pears with Florentines Peel and cut 4 pears in half lengthwise. Scoop out the core with a teaspoon to make a hole. Place in an ovenproof dish and drizzle over the juice of 1 lemon. Mix together ¼ cup packed light brown sugar and 4 tablespoons softened unsalted butter in a bowl and dot over the pears. Place in a preheated oven, at 350°F, for 10 minutes. Remove from the oven and add a crumbled chocolate florentine into each hole, then pour over a 5 oz can evaporated milk and stir. Return to the oven for an additional 10 minutes, stirring the sauce once. Transfer the pears to 4 serving plates and pour over the sauce.

 # Raspberry Millefeuille

Serves 6

12 oz package chilled,
 rolled puff pastry
1¼ cups heavy cream
2 tablespoons raspberry liqueur
 (optional)
2 cups raspberries
confectioners' sugar, for dusting

- Line a large baking sheet with nonstick parchment paper. Unroll the pastry and place on the baking sheet. Prick all over with a fork and cover with another piece of parchment paper. Place a wire rack on top (this prevents the pastry from rising too much).

- Place in a preheated oven, at 425°F, for 10 minutes. Using an oven mitt, carefully remove the wire rack and parchment paper and turn over the pastry. Return to the oven for an additional 5 minutes or until browned. Cool on a wire rack.

- Meanwhile, lightly whip the cream and liqueur, if using, in a bowl with a handheld electric mixer until it forms soft peaks.

- Cut the pastry into 3 even strips. Place 1 strip of pastry on a large serving plate and spoon over half the cream and half the raspberries. Repeat the layers, finishing with a layer of pastry. Dust with confectioners' sugar and serve immediately.

 Quick Raspberry Tarts

Lightly whip 1¼ cups heavy cream in a bowl with a handheld electric mixer until it forms soft peaks, then spoon into 6 single-serving, store-bought piecrusts. Top with 2 cups raspberries and dust with confectioners' sugar. Serve immediately.

Individual Raspberry Millefeuilles Unroll a 12 oz package chilled, rolled puff pastry and cut into twelve 3½ inch squares. Place on a baking sheet and bake in a preheated oven, at 425°F, for 12–15 minutes until golden. Let cool. Meanwhile, lightly whip 1¼ cups heavy cream in a bowl with a handheld electric mixer until it forms soft peaks. Spoon the cream over 6 pieces of the pastry, then divide 2 cups raspberries among the squares. Top with the remaining pastry and dust with confectioners' sugar. Serve immediately.

3⬤ Banana and Caramel Tarte Tatin

Serves 6

butter, for greasing

12 oz package chilled, rolled puff pastry

4 ripe bananas, cut in half lengthwise

1¼ cups store-bought caramel sauce

vanilla ice cream or light cream, to serve (optional)

- Lightly grease a 9 inch round cake pan or skillet with an ovenproof handle. Unroll the pastry and cut out a circle slightly larger than the pan or skillet.

- Lay the bananas, cut side down, in the bottom of the pan. Spoon over the caramel sauce, covering the bananas evenly. Place the pastry circle over the pan, tucking the edges loosely around the edges so that steam can escape.

- Place in a preheated oven, at 400°F, for 20–25 minutes or until the pastry is puffed and golden. Let stand for a few minutes to cool slightly.

- Using an oven mitt, place a serving dish on top of the pan and turn upside down. Scrape any remaining sauce over the tarte tatin. Serve immediately with vanilla ice cream or light cream, if using.

1⬤ **Banana Waffles with Caramel Sauce and Pecans** Lightly toast 6 waffles and place in bowls. Slice 6 large bananas and arrange over the top of the waffles, then pour over 1¼ cups warmed store-bought caramel sauce. Sprinkle over ¼ cup chopped pecans. Serve immediately with scoops of vanilla ice cream.

2⬤ **Baked Bananas with Caramel Sauce** Cook 6 large, unpeeled bananas in an ovenproof dish in a preheated oven, at 350°F, for 15–20 minutes or until the skins have blackened and the flesh is soft. Slice the bananas lengthwise, keeping them in their skins, and place in bowls. Drizzle over 1¼ cups warmed store-bought caramel sauce, sprinkle each with some chopped pecans, and serve with a scoop of vanilla ice cream.

30 Brandy Snaps with Limoncello Cream

Serves 6

sunflower oil, for greasing
6 tablespoons unsalted butter
⅓ cup superfine sugar
3 tablespoons light corn syrup
⅔ cup all-purpose flour
1 teaspoon ground ginger
2 tablespoons brandy
1 tablespoon lemon juice

For the limoncello cream

1 cup heavy cream
3 tablespoons limoncello liqueur

- Lightly oil the handles of several wooden spoons and line 4 large baking sheets with nonstick parchment paper.

- Place the butter, sugar, and light corn syrup in a heavy saucepan and warm gently over medium heat until the mixture is combined. Let cool for 2–3 minutes, then stir in the flour, ginger, brandy, and lemon juice. Mix until smooth.

- Place tablespoons of the mixture onto the prepared baking sheets, allowing plenty of room for spreading, to make 12–16 brandy snaps. Place 2 sheets at a time in a preheated oven, at 375°F, for 8–10 minutes or until golden.

- Let cool on the sheets for 10–15 seconds, then loosen a brandy snap with a spatula and roll around a spoon handle. Transfer to a wire rack to harden. Repeat with the remaining brandy snaps, returning to the oven for a few moments to soften if they set too hard.

- Lightly whip the cream and limoncello in a bowl with a handheld electric mixer and spoon or pipe into the brandy snaps. Serve immediately.

1 Limoncello Brandy Snap Baskets

Make the limoncello cream as above. Place 6 store-bought brandy snap baskets on plates and fill with the lemon cream. Top with 1 cup raspberries and serve immediately.

2 Chocolate-Dipped Limoncello Brandy

Snaps Melt 2 oz semisweet dark or milk chocolate, broken into small pieces, in a heatproof bowl set over a saucepan of gently simmering water. Remove from the heat and dip each end of 12 store-bought brandy snaps into the melted chocolate. Transfer to a wire rack to set. Make the limoncello cream as above. Once set, fill the brandy snaps with the cream and serve 2 per person.

Banana and Irish Cream Trifles

Serves 4

1 cup mascarpone cheese

6 tablespoons Irish cream liqueur

7 oz store-bought banana
  loaf cake, cubed

3 bananas, sliced

¼ cup store-bought
  caramel sauce

1¼ cups store-bought vanilla
  pudding or freshly prepared
  custard (see page 150)

¼ cup chopped pecans

- Beat together the mascarpone and 2 tablespoons of the liqueur in a bowl and chill.

- Meanwhile, divide the cake among 4 glasses, then drizzle each with 1 tablespoon of the liqueur. Add the bananas, reserving 4 slices for decoration, then drizzle each with ½ tablespoon of the caramel sauce. Spoon over the pudding and top with the mascarpone cream.

- Drizzle with the remaining caramel sauce and decorate with the reserved banana slices and pecans. Serve immediately.

2 **Banana, Irish Cream, and Caramel Pudding** Slice an 8 oz store-bought banana loaf cake and arrange in the bottom of a 1 quart ovenproof dish. Drizzle over 2 tablespoons Irish cream liqueur. Top with 2 sliced bananas and ¼ cup chopped pecans, then pour over 1 cup store-bought caramel sauce. Place in a preheated oven, at 350°F, for 15 minutes or until bubbling.

3 **Banana and Irish Cream Custard** Pour 1¼ cups milk into a saucepan and place over medium heat. Add a split vanilla bean and bring the milk to a boil. Place 3 egg yolks, 1 tablespoon cornstarch, and 2 tablespoons superfine sugar in a heatproof bowl and beat with a handheld electric mixer until pale and thick. Strain the hot milk onto the egg mixture, beating continuously until well combined. Return to the pan and heat gently over low heat, stirring continuously, until thick enough to coat the back of a spoon. Slice the bananas into the custard and stir to combine. Stir in 2 tablespoons Irish cream liqueur. Pour the hot banana custard into 4 bowls and serve hot or cold, sprinkled with some chopped pecans and grated chocolate.

Chocolate Cups with Mint Syllabub

Serves 6

5 oz semisweet dark chocolate, broken into small pieces
mint leaves, to decorate
unsweetened cocoa powder, for dusting

For the mint syllabub

⅓ cup crème de menthe liqueur
2 tablespoons superfine sugar
1 tablespoon lime juice
1¼ cups heavy cream

- To make the chocolate cups, melt the chocolate in a heatproof bowl set over a saucepan of gently simmering water. Draw six 5 inch circles on wax paper and cut out ½ inch outside the lines. (Do not use parchment paper, because the chocolate will run too much).

- Place 6 upturned, narrow glasses or cups on a baking sheet. Spoon half the melted chocolate onto 3 of the wax circles. Using a teaspoon, spread the chocolate within the drawn circles, making an attractive fluted edge.

- Lift each circle over a glass so that it falls loosely around the sides. Repeat to make 3 more baskets. Chill for 15–20 minutes until firm. Carefully remove the wax paper and chill the baskets again.

- Meanwhile, to make the mint syllabub, place the liqueur, sugar, and lime juice in a bowl and beat with a handheld electric mixer, then beat in the cream until it forms soft peaks.

- Spoon the syllabub into the chilled chocolate cups and serve immediately, decorated with mint leaves and dusted with a little cocoa powder.

Quick Chocolate and Mint Syllabubs

Crush 6 plain chocolate cookies and divide among 6 glasses. Make the mint syllabub as above, then spoon over the cookies. Serve topped with a little grated semisweet dark chocolate and serve immediately.

White Chocolate and Peppermint Mousse Melt 8 oz white chocolate, broken into small pieces, in a heatproof bowl set over a saucepan of gently simmering water, then let cool slightly. Lightly whip 1 cup heavy cream in a bowl with a handheld electric mixer until it forms soft peaks. Stir in ¼–½ teaspoon peppermint extract. Beat 2 egg whites in a clean bowl with a handheld electric mixer until they form soft peaks. Stir a little of the melted chocolate into the cream mixture, then fold in the rest of the chocolate mixture and egg whites. Spoon into 6 glasses and place in the freezer for 5–10 minutes before serving.

 Portuguese Custard Tarts

Serves 8

1 tablespoon instant vanilla
   pudding mix
2 tablespoons superfine sugar
4 egg yolks
scant 1 cup milk
grated rind of 1 lemon
scant 1 cup crème fraîche
½ teaspoon vanilla extract
12 oz package chilled,
   rolled puff pastry
½ teaspoon ground cinnamon
¼ cup store-bought caramel
   sauce, to serve

- Place the vanilla pudding mix, sugar, and egg yolks in a bowl, then add a little of the milk and stir to form a smooth paste. Beat in the remaining milk, then pour into a saucepan and add the lemon rind and crème fraîche.

- Cook over medium heat, beating continuously, for 3–4 minutes until the custard has thickened. Remove from the heat and beat in the vanilla extract. Let cool slightly.

- Unroll the pastry and cut out 8 circles using a 3½ inch cutter, rerolling the trimmings if necessary. Push into 8 cups of a 12-cup nonstick muffin pan, pinching up the edges of the pastry.

- Pour the custard into the pastry shells until nearly full. Place in a preheated oven, at 400°F, for 15–20 minutes or until the pastry is golden and the filling puffed up. Let cool in the pan for a few minutes.

- Turn out the tarts onto serving plates, drizzle over the caramel sauce, and serve immediately.

1 Quick Creamy Custard

Pour a 12 oz can evaporated milk into a saucepan and stir in 1 teaspoon vanilla extract and 2 tablespoons superfine sugar. Blend 2 tablespoons instant vanilla pudding mix with ¼ cup cold water in a bowl to form a paste. Add the vanilla paste to the pan and cook over low heat, beating continuously, until the custard has boiled and thickened. Serve poured over crisps and pies.

2 Nutmeg and Custard Tarts

Heat 1¼ cups light cream in a saucepan until lukewarm. Place 3 egg yolks and ¼ cup superfine sugar in a heatproof bowl and beat with a handheld electric mixer until creamy, then beat in the warm cream. Strain into a pitcher. Place 8 single-serving, store-bought piecrusts on a baking sheet and pour in the custard. Sprinkle with grated nutmeg and place in a preheated oven, at 350°F, for 12–15 minutes or until set.

Mini Baked Alaskas

Serves 6

6 slices of store-bought pound cake, cut into ½ inch thick slices

⅔ cup raspberries

1 tablespoon confectioners' sugar

1 tablespoon sherry (optional)

6 scoops of vanilla ice cream

4 egg whites

1 cup superfine sugar

- Line a baking sheet with nonstick parchment paper. Using a 3 inch cutter, stamp out the pound cake to make 6 circles and place on the baking sheet.

- Place the raspberries, confectioners' sugar, and sherry, if using, in a bowl and coarsely mash with a fork. Spoon the crushed raspberries and any juice evenly over the top of the cake circles. Place a scoop of ice cream on top of each cake, then place in the freezer while you make the meringue.

- Beat the egg whites in a clean, large bowl with a handheld electric mixer until stiff, then gradually beat in the sugar until the mixture is thick and glossy.

- Remove the cake circles from the freezer, then quickly cover the ice cream and cake with the meringue. Place in a preheated oven, at 425°F, for 3–4 minutes or until the meringue has browned. Serve immediately.

Raspberry and Ice Cream Baked Meringue Puddings Divide 3½ cups raspberries among six 1 cup ramekins or ovenproof dishes. Beat 3 extra-large egg whites in a clean bowl with a handheld electric mixer until stiff, then gradually beat in ¾ cup superfine sugar until the mixture is thick and glossy. Place 1 scoop of vanilla ice cream in each dish and cover with the meringue. Place on a baking sheet and bake in a preheated oven, at 425°F, for 3–4 minutes or until browned. Serve immediately.

Chocolate and Raspberry Baked Alaska Line a deep, round mold with plastic wrap and spoon in 4 cups good-quality, slightly softened chocolate ice cream. Scatter with 1 cup raspberries and spoon over 2 tablespoons store-bought chocolate sauce. Cover with 3 halved, store-bought chocolate brownies and press down. Place in the freezer for 20 minutes until firm. Meanwhile, beat 3 egg whites in a clean bowl with a handheld electric mixer until stiff, then gradually beat in ⅔ cup superfine sugar until the mixture is thick and glossy. Turn out the ice cream bombe onto an ovenproof plate, remove the plastic wrap, and cover with the meringue. Place in a preheated oven, at 425°F, for 3–4 minutes or until the meringue has browned. Serve immediately.

Coconut and Lime Gelatins

Serves 4

1 envelope lime gelatin
½ cup boiling water
finely grated rind and juice
  of 2 limes
1¾ cups coconut milk, chilled
¼ coconut, white flesh cut into
  thin slithers, to serve

- Place the gelatin in a heatproof pitcher and pour over the measured water. Stir until it is fully dissolved. Stir in the lime rind and juice, then whisk in the coconut milk.

- Pour into four ⅔ cup metal molds, cover with plastic wrap, and place in the freezer for 25 minutes until set. If not serving immediately, remove the gelatins from the freezer and place in the refrigerator.

- Meanwhile, place the coconut in a skillet and dry-fry over medium heat until golden.

- To turn out the gelatins, dip the bottom of the molds in warm water and invert onto serving plates. Serve with the toasted coconut.

---

1   Lime and Coconut Creams

Place ⅔ cup unsweetened coconut cream (look for in Asian grocery stores), the grated rind and juice of 1 lime, 1 cup Greek yogurt, and ¼ cup confectioners' sugar in a bowl and beat together. Spoon into 4 glasses and serve immediately.

2   Coconut and Lime Sponge Puddings

Place ¼ cup superfine sugar, 4 tablespoons softened, unsalted butter, and the finely grated rind of 1 lime in a bowl and beat together with a handheld electric mixer until light and fluffy. Beat in 1 egg and the juice of 1 lime. Gently fold in ⅔ cup self-rising flour and ¾ cup dried shredded coconut. Spoon into 4 greased cups of a 6-cup nonstick muffin pan and place in a preheated oven, at 350°F, for 12–15 minutes until risen and golden. Serve with whipped cream or yogurt.

 # Orange and Rosemary Polenta Cake

Serves 6–8

12 tablespoons (1½ sticks)
   unsalted butter, softened
heaping ¾ cup superfine sugar
finely grated rind and juice
   of 1 orange
1½ cups ground almonds
2 extra-large eggs
½ cup polenta or coarse cornmeal
½ teaspoon baking powder

For the orange syrup

grated rind and juice of
   1 large orange
¼ cup superfine sugar
2 tablespoons water
1 tablespoon chopped rosemary

- Line an 8 inch round cake pan with nonstick parchment paper. Place the butter, sugar, and orange rind in a large bowl and beat with a handheld electric mixer until light and fluffy. Add the ground almonds and eggs and beat well. Stir in the orange juice, polenta, and baking powder and mix until well combined.

- Spoon the mixture into the prepared cake pan and place in a preheated oven, at 350°F, for 20–25 minutes until risen and firm to the touch.

- Meanwhile, place all the syrup ingredients in a saucepan and bring to a boil. Reduce the heat and simmer for 2–3 minutes.

- Spoon the syrup over the cake in the pan, then turn out and serve in slices.

 Oranges in Rosemary Syrup

Place 1 cup superfine sugar, 1 cup water, and 1 rosemary sprig in a saucepan and bring to a boil, stirring until the sugar has dissolved. Reduce the heat and simmer for 5 minutes. Cool slightly, then strain the syrup over 6 peeled and sliced oranges.

Orange Polenta Cakes

Place 6 tablespoons softened unsalted butter, ⅓ cup superfine sugar, and the finely grated rind of ½ orange in a bowl and beat with a handheld electric mixer until light and fluffy, then beat in ½ cup ground almonds, 1 egg, ¾ cup polenta or coarse cornmeal, and ½ teaspoon

baking powder. Spoon into a greased and bottom-lined 6-cup nonstick muffin pan and place in a preheated oven, at 350°F, for 12–15 minutes until risen and firm to the touch. Meanwhile, make the orange syrup as above. Remove the cakes from the muffin pan and spoon over the syrup to serve.

Meringues with Rosewater and Pomegranate

Serves 6

1 cup heavy cream

2 teaspoons rosewater

2 tablespoons confectioners' sugar

a few drops of pink food coloring (optional)

6 meringue nests

¼ cup pomegranate seeds

¼ cup pistachio nuts, coarsely chopped

- Place the cream, rosewater, confectioners' sugar, and food coloring, if using, in a bowl and beat together with a handheld electric mixer until it forms soft peaks.

- Spoon the cream into the meringue nests, then sprinkle each with a handful of the pomegranate seeds. Scatter over the pistachios and serve.

---

2 Rosewater and Pomegranate with Meringues

Place 2 cups heavy cream, 2 teaspoons rosewater, 2 tablespoons confectioners' sugar, and a little pink food coloring (optional) in a bowl and beat together with a handheld electric mixer until it forms soft peaks. Gently stir in 8 coarsely crushed meringue nests and ½ cup pomegranate seeds, reserving a few for decoration. Pile into 6 glasses and decorate with the reserved pomegranate seeds and ½ cup chopped pistachios. Chill for 10 minutes before serving.

3 Pistachio and Rosewater Meringue Roulade

Beat 5 egg whites in a clean, large bowl with a handheld electric mixer until stiff, then gradually beat in 1 cup plus 2 tablespoons superfine sugar until the mixture is thick and glossy. Gently fold in ½ teaspoon white wine vinegar, 1 teaspoon cornstarch, ½ teaspoon vanilla extract, and ½ cup chopped pistachios. Spread the mixture into an 8 x 12 inch jelly roll pan lined with nonstick parchment paper. Place in the center of a preheated oven, at 350°F,  for 15 minutes. Let cool in the pan for 5 minutes. Turn out the meringue onto another piece of parchment paper. Whip together 1¼ cups heavy cream, 2 teaspoons rosewater, and 1 tablespoon confectioners' sugar in a bowl with a handheld electric mixer until it forms soft peaks. Spread evenly over the meringue and scatter over ½ cup pomegranate seeds. Roll up the meringue, transfer to a serving plate, and serve immediately.

Black Currant Galettes

Serves 4

12 oz package chilled,
  rolled puff pastry
1 tablespoon unsalted butter,
  melted
3 tablespoons granulated sugar
2 tablespoons chopped
  mint leaves
2¼ cups black currants
  or blueberries
heavy cream, to serve (optional)

· Unroll the pastry and cut out four 4 inch circles using a fluted cutter. Transfer to a baking sheet and prick with a fork, leaving a ½ inch border. Brush the melted butter over the edges of the pastry.

· Place the sugar and mint in a food processor and blend to form a bright green sugar.

· Scatter the black currants or blueberries over the pastry circles within the borders, then sprinkle over half the mint sugar. Place in a preheated oven, at 425°F, for 15–20 minutes or until risen and golden.

· Sprinkle the galettes with the remaining mint sugar and serve with heavy cream, if using.

1 Black Currant and Cassis Coulis

Place ¼ cup superfine sugar and 2 tablespoons black currant or blueberry syrup in a saucepan. Stir in 1 cup black currants or blueberries and heat gently until the sugar has dissolved. Simmer gently for 3–4 minutes until the fruit is soft. Place in a food processor or blender and blend to a puree, then, if using black currants, press through a strainer to remove any seeds. Serve over ice cream or fruit.

2 Black Currant and Mint Fools

Place 3 cups black currants or blueberries, ½ cup superfine sugar, and 2 tablespoons black currant or blueberry syrup in a large saucepan and simmer gently for 5–6 minutes until the fruit is soft. Place in a food processor or blender and blend to a puree, then, if using black currants, press through a strainer to remove the seeds. Lightly whip ⅔ cup heavy cream in a large bowl with a handheld electric mixer until it forms soft peaks, then fold in ⅔ cup Greek yogurt, 2 tablespoons chopped mint, and the puree. Spoon into 4 glasses and serve immediately.

 # Lavender Crème Brûlées

Serves 6

3 egg yolks

1 tablespoon instant
 vanilla pudding mix

3 tablespoons lavender sugar

1¼ cups milk

1¼ cups mascarpone cheese

⅔ cup superfine sugar

- Chill six ½ cup ramekins while you make the filling. Place the egg yolks, vanilla pudding powder, lavender sugar, and 3 tablespoons of the milk in a heatproof bowl and beat together.

- Meanwhile, warm the remaining milk in a saucepan. Gradually beat into the egg mixture. Return to the pan and cook, beating continuously, over medium heat for 3–4 minutes until the mixture has thickened. Let cool slightly. Beat in half of the mascarpone until smooth, then beat in the remaining mascarpone.

- Pour the mixture into the ramekins and place in the freezer for 15 minutes.

- Place the superfine sugar in a small, heavy saucepan over low heat and let heat until half of it has melted and started to color, then gently stir it. Keep stirring until it has turned a deep golden caramel color. Drizzle a little over the top of each ramekin. Let cool for a few minutes until the caramel has hardened, then serve.

---

1 **Quick Lavender and Fruit Crème Brûlées**

Spoon 1½ cups store-bought fruit compote, such as mixed berries, into six 6 ⅔ cup ramekins. Spoon 3 cups Greek yogurt over the compote, then sprinkle the tops with ⅔ cup lavender sugar. Place on a baking sheet and cook under a preheated hot broiler for 4–5 minutes or until the sugar is brown and bubbling. Let stand for 3–4 minutes before serving.

2 **Lavender Cookies**

Place ⅔ cup all-purpose flour, 4 tablespoons chilled, diced unsalted butter, and 2 tablespoons lavender sugar in a food processor and blend until the mixture comes together to form a dough. Turn out onto a lightly floured surface and roll out to ¼ inch thick, then cut into 12 circles using a 1¾ inch fluted cutter. Place on a baking sheet lined with nonstick parchment paper and bake in a preheated oven, at 350°F, for 10–12 minutes. Serve 2 cookies per person with Greek yogurt.

Hot Mango and Passion Fruit Soufflés

Serves 6

butter, for greasing
¼ cup superfine sugar, plus
  2 tablespoons for dusting
½ cup canned mango puree
3 passion fruit, pulp strained
  to remove the seeds
1 tablespoon cornstarch
2 tablespoons cold water
confectioners' sugar, for dusting

For the meringue

5 egg whites
⅓ cup superfine sugar

- Grease six 1 cup ramekins or soufflé dishes, then dust with the 2 tablespoons sugar to cover the bottom and sides. Place on a baking sheet.

- Place the mango, passion fruit, and the ¼ cup sugar in a saucepan over low heat and stir until the sugar has dissolved, then bring to a boil. Blend the cornstarch with the measured water in a bowl to form a paste. Add to the mango in the pan and cook for 1 minute, stirring continuously. Pour into a large bowl and chill.

- Meanwhile, beat the egg whites in a clean, large bowl with a handheld electric mixer until stiff, then gradually beat in the sugar until the mixture is thick and glossy. Gently fold the meringue into the chilled mango.

- Spoon into the prepared dishes and spread the tops level, then clean the edges with a fingertip. Place in a preheated oven, at 350°F, for 10–12 minutes or until risen and golden. Dust with confectioners' sugar and serve immediately.

---

1 Passion Fruit Syrup
Place 1 cup superfine sugar, 1 cup water, and the seeds and pulp of 6 passion fruit in a saucepan and cook over low heat, stirring, until the sugar has dissolved. Increase the heat and let the mixture boil for 5–6 minutes until syrupy. Serve poured over mango sorbet.

3 Passion Fruit and Mango Millefeuille
Brush 3 large sheets of phyllo pastry with 2 tablespoons melted, unsalted butter to stick them together, then cut into 5 x 2 inch rectangles. Place on a baking sheet and cook in preheated oven, at 350°F, for 5–7 minutes or until golden. Transfer to a cooling rack and let cool for 10 minutes. Meanwhile, lightly whip 1 cup heavy cream in a bowl with a handheld electric mixer until it forms soft peaks, then stir in the pulp of 2 passion fruit and 3 tablespoons canned mango puree. Transfer to a bowl and chill for 10 minutes. Spoon the cream onto 6 of the phyllo rectangles, then top with the remaining pastry rectangles. Dust with confectioners' sugar before serving.

30 Mini Baked Cappuccino Cheesecakes

Serves 6

1⅓ cups crushed amaretti cookies

2 tablespoons unsalted butter, melted

2 teaspoons espresso powder

2 tablespoons boiling water

⅓ cup superfine sugar

1 teaspoon vanilla extract

1 cup light cream cheese

1 tablespoon cornstarch

2 eggs

⅔ cup whipping cream

unsweetened cocoa powder, for dusting

- Line a 6-cup muffin pan with paper liners. Stir the crushed cookies into the melted butter and press into the bottom of the paper liners. Chill while you make the filling.

- Place the espresso powder in a heatproof bowl and pour over the measured water to dissolve. Let cool.

- Place the sugar, vanilla extract, cream cheese, cornstarch, and eggs in a bowl and beat together until smooth, then stir in the espresso.

- Spoon the mixture over the cookie crusts and place in a preheated oven, at 325°F, for 15 minutes. Let cool in the pan for 5 minutes.

- Remove the cheesecakes from the liners and place on 6 serving plates. Lightly whip the cream in a bowl with a handheld electric mixer until it forms soft peaks, then spoon on top of the warm cheesecakes. Dust with the cocoa powder and serve.

 Coffee Meringues

Dissolve 2 teaspoons espresso powder in 2 tablespoons boiling water in a heatproof bowl and let cool. Lightly whip 1¼ cups heavy cream and the espresso in a bowl with a handheld electric mixer until it forms soft peaks. Sandwich together 24 mini meringue shells with the coffee cream. Serve 2 meringues per person, dusted with unsweetened cocoa powder.

 Mascarpone and Coffee Creams

Dissolve 4 teaspoons espresso powder in 3 tablespoons boiling water in a heatproof bowl and let cool. Lightly crush 18 amaretti cookies and divide half among 6 glasses. Place 1¼ cups mascarpone cheese, 3 tablespoons confectioners' sugar, and the espresso in a bowl and beat with a handheld electric mixer until smooth. Beat in 1¼ cups heavy cream until creamy, then spoon into the glasses. Top with the remaining cookies and serve.

 Chocolate Zabaglione

Serves 6

12 amaretti cookies
2 tablespoons Marsala

For the zabaglione
¼ cup unsweetened cocoa
  powder, sifted, plus extra
  for dusting
5 egg yolks
¼ cup superfine sugar
⅔ cup Marsala

- Divide the cookies among 6 tall, stemmed glasses. Spoon 1 teaspoon of the Marsala over each.

- To make the zabaglione, put the cocoa powder, egg yolks, and sugar in a large heatproof bowl set over a saucepan of simmering water. Beat with a handheld electric mixer until smooth, then gradually beat in the remaining Marsala. Continue beating for an additional 8–10 minutes or until the mixture is slightly paler in color, has increased in volume, and is foamy.

- Carefully spoon the mixture into the glasses. Dust with cocoa powder and serve immediately.

 **Sweet Marsala Creams**

Place ¼ cup superfine sugar, 1 egg, and 1 extra egg yolk in a bowl and beat with a handheld electric mixer until it forms soft ribbons. Beat in 1 cup mascarpone cheese and 2 tablespoons Marsala. Lightly whip 1 cup heavy whipping cream in a separate bowl with a handheld electric mixer until it forms soft peaks, then fold into the mascarpone. Pour the cream mixture into 6 small glasses and scatter with 1 oz grated semisweet dark chocolate. Serve with amaretti cookies.

Marsala and Chocolate Tart

Melt 8 oz semisweet dark chocolate (85 percent cocoa solids), broken into small pieces, in a heatproof bowl set over a saucepan of gently simmering water, then let cool slightly. Place 2 extra-large eggs, ¼ cup superfine sugar, and 3 tablespoons Marsala in a bowl and beat with a handheld electric mixer until pale and fluffy. Beat in the chocolate until well combined. Place an 8 inch store-bought piecrust on a baking sheet. Pour in the chocolate mixture and spread the top level. Place in a preheated oven, at 325°F, for 10–12 minutes or until just set. The mixture should be slightly wobbly in the center, but it will continue to set on cooling. Let stand for 10 minutes, then serve with Marsala-flavored heavy cream.

30 Parmesan and Rosemary Thins with Poached Grapes

Serves 6

1 cup Muscat
  sweet wine
½ cup honey
3½ cups seedless red grapes

For the cookies

⅔ cup all-purpose flour,
  plus extra for dusting
4 tablespoons unsalted butter,
  diced
½ cup finely grated Parmesan
  cheese
1 teaspoon ground black pepper
½ teaspoon salt
1 tablespoon chopped rosemary

· To make the cookies, place the flour in a bowl, add the butter, and rub in with the fingertips until the mixture resembles fine bread crumbs. Alternatively, use a food processor. Add the Parmesan, black pepper, salt, and rosemary and mix in thoroughly. Bring the mixture together to form a dough.

· Turn the dough out onto a lightly floured surface and knead briefly. Roll out to ⅛ inch thick and cut out cookies using a 2½ inch cutter. Place onto a large nonstick baking sheet and bake on the top shelf of a preheated oven, at 325°F, for 10 minutes. Carefully turn the cookies over, then return to the oven for an additional 5 minutes or until golden brown on both sides. Let cool on the sheet for 5 minutes, then turn out onto a wire rack to cool completely.

· Meanwhile, pour the wine into a small saucepan and add the honey. Bring to a boil, then reduce the heat and simmer for 10 minutes until syrupy. Add the grapes and simmer for 3–4 minutes. Let cool for 2 minutes.

· Spoon the grapes into 6 glasses and serve with the cookies.

1 Grape and Orange-Blossom Honey

Fruit Salad Halve 3½ cups seedless red and green grapes and place in a bowl. Mix together 3 tablespoons orange-blossom honey and 3 tablespoons orange juice in a bowl, then pour over the grapes. Spoon into 6 small bowls and serve with spoonfuls of vanilla yogurt.

2 Grapes Poached in Rosemary Syrup

Place ½ cup superfine sugar, ⅔ cup water, and 2 rosemary sprigs in a saucepan over medium heat and bring to a boil, stirring until the sugar has dissolved. Reduce the heat and simmer for 5 minutes. Add 4 cups seedless grapes and simmer gently for an additional 5–10 minutes until soft. Remove the rosemary and serve the grapes with the syrup and Greek yogurt.

DES-ENTE-JYX

QuickCook
Healthy Options

Recipes listed by cooking time

30

20

 # Frozen Berry Yogurt Ice Cream

Serves 4

2½ cups frozen mixed berries, such as raspberries, blueberries, and strawberries

1 cup fat-free Greek yogurt

2 tablespoons confectioners' sugar

thin cookies, to serve

· Place half the berries, the yogurt, and confectioners' sugar in a food processor or blender and blend until fairly smooth and the berries have broken up.

· Add the rest of the berries and blend until they are slightly broken up but some texture remains. Place scoops of the yogurt ice cream into bowls and serve immediately with cookies, if using.

---

2 **Frozen Berry Yogurt Ice Cream Sundaes** Place 1 cup raspberries and 1 tablespoon confectioners' sugar in a food processor or blender and blend to make a smooth coulis, then strain to remove the seeds. Make the yogurt ice cream as above. Break up 4 meringue nests and divide half among 4 glasses. Add 1 scoop of the yogurt ice cream to each glass, then pour over a little of the coulis. Repeat the layers, finishing with the coulis. Serve immediately.

3 **Frozen Berry Yogurt Ice Cream in Lemon Tuile Baskets** Beat 1 egg white in a clean bowl with a handheld electric mixer until stiff, then gradually beat in ¼ cup superfine sugar until thick and glossy. Fold in 2 tablespoons melted and cooled, unsalted butter, the rind of ½ lemon, and 3 tablespoons all-purpose flour. Place tablespoons of the mixture, spaced well apart, onto each of 2 lightly greased nonstick baking sheets. Spread out to 5 inch circles. Place one baking sheet at a time in a preheated oven, at 350°F, for 5–6 minutes or until golden around the edges. Carefully drape the cookies over upturned, oiled single-serving ramekins or molds to form baskets and let cool. Meanwhile, make the yogurt ice cream as above. Serve the tuile baskets filled with scoops of the ice cream.

 Easy Blackberry Fool

Serves 4

2 cups blackberries, plus extra
  to decorate
¼ cup confectioners' sugar
1 tablespoon lemon juice
1 cup mascarpone cheese
1 cup fat-free Greek yogurt

- Place the blackberries, confectioners' sugar, and lemon juice in a food processor or blender and blend to a puree, then press through a strainer into a large bowl to remove the seeds. Beat in the mascarpone and yogurt.

- Spoon into 4 glass dishes and chill for 10 minutes. Decorate with extra blackberries before serving.

---

1 **Blackberry Coulis**
Place 1¾ cups blackberries, ¼ cup superfine sugar, and ½ cup water in a small saucepan and bring to a boil. Reduce the heat and simmer for 5 minutes until the fruit is soft. Stir in ½ teaspoon vanilla extract. Turn into a food processor or blender and blend to a puree, then press through a strainer into a bowl, rubbing it through with the back of a ladle or spoon. Serve warm or chilled with fat-free Greek yogurt.

3 **Blackberry Upside-Down Cake** Lightly grease and line the bottom of an 8 inch springform round cake pan with nonstick parchment paper. Scatter 2½ cups blackberries over the bottom and sprinkle over 2 tablespoons superfine sugar. Place 2 eggs, ⅓ cup superfine sugar, and the grated rind of 1 lemon in a large bowl and beat with a handheld electric mixer until pale and thick and the beaters leave a trail when lifted above the mixture. Gently stir in the juice of 1 lemon and fold in ⅔ cup self-rising flour. Pour over the blackberries and place in a preheated oven, at 350°F, for 20–25 minutes or until golden brown and firm to the touch. Let cool in the pan for a few minutes, then invert onto a plate. Serve with fat-free Greek yogurt.

Grilled Peaches and Apricots with Honey Yogurt

Serves 4

2 tablespoons vanilla sugar

3 peaches, halved, pitted, and cut into quarters

4 apricots, halved and pitted

1 cup fat-free Greek yogurt

2 tablespoons honey

- Place the sugar in a large bowl, then add the fruit and toss gently to coat.

- Preheat a ridged grill pan until hot, then add the peaches, cut side down, and cook over medium heat for 2–3 minutes until caramelized, then add the apricots. Turn over the peaches and cook for an additional 2–3 minutes or until the apricots and peaches are soft.

- Meanwhile, place the yogurt in a bowl and pour over the honey. Stir to create a rippled effect. Serve the warmed fruit with the honey yogurt.

---

2 **Oven-Roasted Cinnamon Peaches and Apricots** Halve and pit 3 peaches and cut into quarters, then halve and pit 3 apricots and place cut side up in an ovenproof dish. Mix together 3 tablespoons light brown sugar and 1 teaspoon ground cinnamon in a bowl and sprinkle over the fruit. Place in a preheated oven, at 400°F, for 10–15 minutes or until softened and starting to caramelize. Serve with dollops of fat-free yogurt.

3 **Poached Vanilla Peaches** Dunk 4 ripe peaches into a heatproof bowl of boiling water for 1 minute, then place in a bowl of cold water and slip off the skins. Place in a saucepan that holds them snugly, then pour over 1 cup water. Split open 1 vanilla bean and scrape out the seeds. Mix the seeds with ½ cup superfine sugar in a bowl and sprinkle over the peaches, placing the vanilla bean in the middle. Cover with a lid and cook for 20–25 minutes, turning once and stirring to dissolve the sugar. Serve warm with some syrup poured over.

Carpaccio of Pineapple with Basil

Serves 4

1 supersweet pineapple, chilled
2 tablespoons honey
juice of ½ lime
2 teaspoons freshly ground
  black pepper
6 large basil leaves, shredded

- Cut the top and bottom off the pineapple. Hold the pineapple firmly, resting it on the cut bottom. Slice off the skin, working from top to bottom, removing any brown "eyes." Halve lengthwise, remove the tough core in the center using an apple corer, and cut into thin slices. Arrange on a large serving platter.

- Mix together the honey, lime juice, and black pepper in a small bowl and drizzle over the pineapple. Scatter over the basil and serve immediately.

1 Pineapple and Basil Sorbet

Place 3 cups frozen pineapple chunks, 2 tablespoons superfine sugar, and 2 tablespoons lime juice in a food processor and blend until the pineapple starts to break down. Add 2 tablespoons freshly chopped basil and blend for 2–3 minutes until the mixture starts to come together. Spoon into 4 bowls and serve immediately.

3 Pineapple and Basil Kebabs

Skin and core 1 pineapple as above and cut into 1 inch cubes. Place in a large bowl and stir in 3 tablespoons honey, 1 tablespoon freshly chopped basil, and the grated rind and juice of 1 lime. Let marinate for 15 minutes, then thread onto 8 metal skewers. Cook under a preheated hot broiler or on a barbecue for 3–4 minutes on each side or until lightly golden. Serve 2 kebabs per person.

DES-HEAL-XAF

 **Balsamic and Black Pepper Strawberries**

Serves 4

3½ cups strawberries,
hulled and halved
2 tablespoons balsamic vinegar
1 teaspoon freshly ground
black pepper

- Place the strawberries in a bowl and pour over the vinegar.
- Stir well, to incorporate the flavors, then add the black pepper to taste. Serve immediately.

2 **Strawberry and Black Pepper**

Sauce Place 3½ cups hulled strawberries and 2 tablespoons confectioners' sugar in a food processor or blender and blend until the sauce is smooth. Transfer to a pitcher and stir in 1–2 teaspoons freshly ground black pepper. Chill for 10 minutes, then serve poured over frozen yogurt.

3 **Baked Balsamic and Black Pepper**

Strawberry Bundles
Mix together 1½ lb hulled strawberries, ½ cup balsamic vinegar, 2 tablespoons superfine sugar, and 1 teaspoon black pepper in a large bowl. Divide among 4 double thickness 10 inch aluminum foil squares, folding in the edges to seal. Place the bundles on a baking sheet and bake in a preheated oven, at 325°F, for 25 minutes.

 Pistachio and Orange-Blossom Oranges

Serves 4

4 large oranges

2–3 teaspoons orange-blossom water

1 tablespoon confectioners' sugar

2 tablespoons coarsely chopped pistachio nuts

- Using a sharp knife, slice the top and bottom off the oranges, then remove the skin and pith. Slice each orange into 6 circles, reserving the juice.

- Mix together the reserved juice, orange slices, orange-blossom water, to taste, and confectioners' sugar in a bowl.

- Divide the orange slices among 4 bowls, then drizzle the juice over each and sprinkle with the pistachios.

---

2 **Pistachio Meringues with Orange-Blossom Water** Place ½ cup Greek yogurt, 1 teaspoon grated orange rind, 1 tablespoon confectioners' sugar, and ½–1 teaspoon orange-blossom water, to taste, in a bowl and stir together. Spoon the mixture into 4 meringue nests. Using a sharp knife, remove the skin and outer pith from 1 orange. Cut between the pith into segments. Top the meringues with a couple of the orange segments and sprinkle over ¼ cup chopped pistachios. Serve immediately.

 3 **Orange and Pistachio Risotto** Place 2½ cups lowfat milk, ¼ cup superfine sugar, and the grated rind of 1 orange in a small saucepan and heat gently to simmering point. Meanwhile, melt 2 tablespoons unsalted butter in a saucepan and stir in 1 cup risotto rice. Mix well to coat the grains in the butter, then add the juice of 1 orange. Bring to a boil, then reduce the heat and simmer for 2–3 minutes. Gradually add the warm milk to the rice, stirring occasionally, until most of it has been absorbed and the rice is slightly al dente with a creamy sauce. This should take about 20–25 minutes. Spoon into 4 bowls and serve sprinkled with ¼ cup chopped pistachios.

 Spiced Dried Fruit Compote

Serves 4

4 dried pears or apple rings
4 dried figs
8 dried apricots
8 dried prunes (dried plums)
2½ cups fresh orange juice
1 cinnamon stick
1 star anise
brown sugar, to taste

To serve (optional)
fat-free Greek yogurt
ground cinnamon

- Place the dried fruits in a saucepan with the orange juice and spices and bring to a boil. Reduce the heat, cover, and simmer for 25–30 minutes until the fruits are plump and tender and the liquid syrupy.

- Check the liquid occasionally during cooking, adding a little water if necessary. Taste the liquid and add a little sugar if required. Remove the spices.

- Spoon into 4 bowls and serve with spoonfuls of fat-free Greek yogurt sprinkled with a little ground cinnamon, if liked.

1 Prune and Apple Compote

Place 25 dried prunes (dried plums) and 1¼ cups apple juice in a saucepan and bring to a boil. Reduce the heat and simmer for 8–10 minutes until the prunes are plump and the liquid syrupy. Serve with fat-free Greek yogurt.

2 Tropical Fruit Compote

Place ¼ cup superfine sugar, a strip of lemon peel, and 2½ cups cold water in a saucepan and bring to a boil, stirring until the sugar has dissolved, then boil the syrup for 10 minutes. Add 2 cups dried tropical fruits (such as mango, pineapple, papaya, and melon) to the pan and simmer gently for 5–6 minutes until the fruit is tender. Serve with a little shredded basil.

Ricotta with Warm Cinnamon Honey

Serves 4

2 cups ricotta cheese
½ cup honey
½ teaspoon ground cinnamon
handful of raspberries, to serve

- Line four ½ cup dariole molds with plastic wrap. Press the ricotta into the molds, then place in the freezer for 5 minutes.

- Meanwhile, gently warm the honey and cinnamon in a small saucepan.

- Remove the ricotta molds from the freezer and invert onto plates. Remove the plastic wrap and pour over the warm syrup. Serve with a few raspberries.

2 Ricotta and Honey Baked Nectarines

Halve and pit 4 nectarines and place cut side up in an ovenproof dish. Place ½ cup ricotta cheese, 2 tablespoons honey, and ½ teaspoon ground cinnamon in a bowl and beat together. Pile the mixture onto the fruit and place in a preheated oven, at 400°F, for 10–15 minutes or until the fruit is soft. Drizzle with a little extra honey to serve.

3 Baked Ricotta Cakes with Honey

Place 1 cup ricotta cheese in a bowl and break it up with a wooden spoon. Beat 2 egg whites in a clean bowl with a handheld electric mixer until stiff, then fold into the ricotta with ¼ cup honey. Spoon the mixture into 4 greased ½ cup ramekins and spread the tops level. Place on a baking sheet and bake in a preheated oven, at 350°F, for 20 minutes or until risen and golden. Turn out the ricotta cakes onto serving plates and serve drizzled with ¼ cup warmed honey flavored with a pinch of ground cinnamon.

Grilled Mango with Lime and Chili Syrup

Serves 4

4 ripe mangoes

For the lime and chili syrup

1 red chili, seeded and thinly sliced
grated rind and juice of 1 lime
⅔ cup superfine sugar
⅔ cup cold water

- To make the lime and chili syrup, place all the ingredients in a small saucepan and stir over low heat until the sugar has dissolved. Bring to a boil, then reduce the heat and simmer for 8–10 minutes until syrupy.

- Meanwhile, heat a ridged grill pan. Using a sharp knife, remove the skins from the mangoes, then cut each one into thick slices either side of the pit. Place the mango slices on the hot grill pan and cook for 4–5 minutes on each side.

- Transfer to 4 serving plates and serve with the warm syrup drizzled over the top.

2 **Mango, Lime, and Chili Coulis**

Peel, pit, and cut 2 ripe mangoes into chunks, then place in a food processor or blender with 1 seeded and chopped red chili and the grated rind and juice of 2 limes. Blend for 4–5 minutes until smooth. Serve poured over frozen yogurt.

3 **Mango Fruit Salad with Lime and Chili Syrup** Prepare the syrup as above, transfer to a pitcher, and chill for 10–12 minutes. Remove the skins from 2 ripe mangoes using a sharp knife, then cut each one into thin slices either side of the pit. Place in a bowl and pour over the cooled syrup.

Fluffy Lemon Mousse

Serves 4

⅔ cup fat-free Greek yogurt
⅔ cup half-fat crème fraîche
grated rind and juice of
  1 unwaxed lemon
¼ cup superfine sugar
2 egg whites
grated lemon rind,
  to decorate

• Place the yogurt, crème fraîche, lemon rind, and sugar in a large bowl and beat together with a handheld electric mixer until smooth. Add the lemon juice and beat again until the mixture has thickened slightly.

• Beat the egg whites in a clean bowl with a handheld electric mixer until they form soft peaks, then fold into the lemon mixture.

• Spoon the mousse into 4 glasses and chill for 10 minutes. Serve decorated with the lemon rind.

Homemade Creamy Lemon Yogurt

Mix together 2 cups fat-free Greek yogurt and ¼–⅓ cup lemon curd, to taste, in a bowl. Spoon into 4 glasses and serve topped with 1 cup granola.

Lemon Soufflés

Lightly grease four 1 cup ramekins or soufflé dishes, then dust the insides with 2 tablespoons superfine sugar. Place on a baking sheet. Finely grate the rind of 1 lemon and squeeze the juice of 2 lemons to make ½ cup. Place in a the lemon rind and juice in a saucepan with ¼ cup superfine sugar and cook over low heat until the sugar has dissolved, then bring to a boil. Blend 1 tablespoon cornstarch and 2 tablespoons cold water in a bowl to form a paste. Add to the lemon mixture in the pan and cook for 1 minute, stirring continuously until thickened. Transfer to a bowl and chill for 10 minutes. Beat 4 egg whites in a clean, large bowl with a handheld electric mixer until stiff, then gradually beat in ¼ cup superfine sugar until the mixture is thick and glossy. Gently fold the cooled lemon mixture into the meringue. Spoon the mixture into the prepared dishes and spread the tops level, then clean the edges with a fingertip. Place in a preheated oven, at 350°F, for 10–12 minutes until risen and golden. Serve immediately.

DES-HEAL-ROO

Mango, Cardamom, and Mint Fools

Serves 6

2½ cups fat-free
  Greek yogurt, chilled
5 green cardamom pods,
  seeds finely crushed
2 tablespoons confectioners'
  sugar
grated rind and juice of 1 lime
1 cup canned mango puree
2 tablespoons chopped mint

To decorate
chopped mango
mint sprigs

- Place the yogurt, crushed cardamom, confectioners' sugar, and lime rind and juice in a large bowl and slowly beat together with a handheld electric mixer for 1–2 minutes.

- Beat in the mango puree until combined, then stir in the mint. Spoon into 6 glasses and chill for 10 minutes.

- Serve decorated with chopped mango and a mint sprig.

---

1 **Simple Mango and Cardamom Fruit Salad** Peel, pit, and slice 4 mangoes and arrange on a plate. Sprinkle over the crushed powder from 4 green cardamom pods, then grate over the rind of 1 lime and squeeze over the juice. Sprinkle with 2 tablespoons chopped mint and serve immediately.

3 **Mango and Cardamom Upside-Down Cake**
Lightly grease and line the bottom of an 8 inch springform round cake pan with nonstick parchment paper. Arrange 2 peeled, pitted, and sliced mangoes over the bottom and sprinkle with 1 tablespoon light brown sugar. Place 2 eggs and ⅓ cup superfine sugar in a bowl and beat with a handheld electric mixer until pale and thick and the beaters leave a trail when lifted above the mixture. Gently stir in the crushed powder from 4 green cardamom pods, the grated rind of 1 lime, and 1 tablespoon lime juice. Fold in ⅔ cup self-rising flour. Pour over the mangoes and place in a preheated oven, at 350°F, for 20–25 minutes or until golden brown and firm to the touch. Let cool in the pan for a few minutes, then invert onto a plate and serve warm.

30 Blackberry and Apple Puffs

Serves 6

2 tablespoons vegetable oil
⅔ cup all-purpose flour
½ tsp ground cinnamon
pinch of salt
¼ cup superfine sugar,
   plus 1 tablespoon
1 cup milk
2 extra-large eggs
1 cup blackberries
1 small apple, cored
   and cut into thin slices
confectioners' sugar, for dusting

- Liberally brush a 12-cup muffin pan with the oil. Place in a preheated oven, at 350°F, to heat.

- Meanwhile, sift the flour, cinnamon, and salt into a large bowl. Stir in the ¼ cup of sugar, and make a well in the center. Beat together the milk and eggs in a pitcher, then gradually beat into the flour to form a smooth batter.

- Remove the hot muffin pan from the oven and pour in the batter. Add a couple of blackberries in the centers, then top with apple slices and sprinkle with the 1 tablespoon sugar.

- Return to the oven and cook for 20 minutes or until risen, golden, and cooked through. Serve dusted with confectioners' sugar.

---

1 **Blackberry Sauce** Place 2 cups blackberries, 2 tablespoons superfine sugar, and the grated rind and juice of 1 lemon in a saucepan and heat gently for 5–6 minutes until the fruit starts to burst. Serve warm with spoonfuls of vanilla yogurt.

2 **Puffed Apple and Blackberry Pancake Pudding** Melt 2 tablespoons unsalted butter in an 8 inch skillet with an ovenproof handle, add 4 sliced apples, and cook for 2–3 minutes. Sprinkle over 1 tablespoon superfine sugar and 1 tablespoon lemon juice, stirring gently until the sugar has dissolved. Meanwhile, mix together heaping ¾ cup all-purpose flour and 1 tablespoon superfine sugar in a large bowl and make a well in the center. Beat together 4 eggs and ¾ cup milk in a pitcher, then gradually beat into the flour to form a smooth batter. Pour over the apples, then scatter over 1 cup blackberries. Place in a preheated oven, at 425°F, for 15–20 minutes or until puffed and golden. Serve immediately.

 Trio of Grapefruits
with Ginger Syrup

Serves 4

2 pink grapefruits
2 red grapefruits
2 white grapefruits
2 tablespoons chopped mint

For the ginger syrup

$\frac{2}{3}$ cup superfine sugar
2 pieces of preserved ginger in syrup, finely chopped
2 tablespoons preserved ginger syrup (taken from the jar)

• Remove the skin from the grapefruits then, holding over a bowl to collect the juice, use a sharp knife to cut into segments between the pith. Place the segments in a serving bowl and chill.

• To make the ginger syrup, pour the grapefruit juice into a pitcher to make 1 cup, then place in a saucepan with the sugar, preserved ginger, and preserved ginger syrup. Bring to a boil, then reduce the heat and simmer for 8–10 minutes. Transfer to a heatproof pitcher and chill for 10 minutes to cool.

• Pour the cooled syrup over the grapefruit and stir in the mint. Serve immediately.

 Broiled Grapefruit with Ginger and Mint Cut 2 pink or red grapefruits in half and place on a baking sheet cut sides up. Chop 2 pieces of preserved ginger in syrup into small pieces and scatter over the top, then drizzle over 1 tablespoon preserved ginger syrup. Cook under a preheated medium broiler for 5 minutes or until the grapefruit is golden. Serve with chopped mint and a dollop of fat-free Greek yogurt.

 Grapefruit Salad with Warm Ginger Syrup Drain two 15 oz cans grapefruit segments in juice and place in a bowl, reserving 1 cup of the juice. Make the ginger syrup as above using the reserved canned juice. Cool slightly, then pour over the grapefruit. Serve immediately.

Floating Islands with Elderflower Syrup and Berries

Serves 6

6 cups frozen mixed berries
¾ cup superfine sugar
¼ cup elderflower syrup

For the floating islands

2 extra-large egg whites
pinch of salt
¼ cup superfine sugar

- Place the berries, sugar, and syrup in a saucepan and cook over low heat, stirring, until the sugar has dissolved. Simmer for 4–5 minutes until the berries have softened, but still retain their shape.

- To make the floating islands, fill a large skillet with water and bring to a simmer. Beat the egg whites and salt in a clean bowl with a handheld electric mixer until they form soft peaks, then gradually beat in the sugar until the mixture is thick and glossy.

- Drop 6 heaping tablespoons of the meringue mixture into the simmering water, using a spoon to help it slide off. Turn after 30 seconds using a slotted spoon and cook for another 30 seconds. Remove and drain on paper towels.

- Spoon the warm berries and the juice into 6 serving bowls and float a meringue on top.

---

1 **Light Elderflower Cream**

Place 1¼ cup Greek yogurt in a bowl and stir in 2 tablespoons elderflower syrup and 1 tablespoon confectioners' sugar. Serve poured over sliced fresh fruit.

3 **Elderflower-Flavored Poached Nectarines or Peaches**

Dunk 6 whole nectarines or peaches into a heatproof bowl of boiling water for 1 minute, then place in a bowl of cold water and slip off the skins. Place 2 cups elderflower-flavored sparkling water and ⅓ cup superfine sugar in a saucepan that will hold the fruit snugly. Bring to a boil, stirring until the sugar has dissolved. Add the fruit, cover, and simmer gently for 10 minutes. Turn the fruit and poach for another 10 minutes until just tender. Spoon the nectarines or peaches into 6 bowls and pour over the syrup to serve.

 Watermelon with Mint Sugar

Serves 4

2 lb watermelon

¼ cup superfine sugar

½ cup mint leaves

- Remove the skin from the watermelon and cut the flesh into cubes, discarding any seeds. Divide among 4 plates.

- Place the sugar and mint in a food processor and blend to form a bright green sugar.

- Serve the watermelon sprinkled with the mint sugar.

Watermelon and Mint Kebabs

Remove the skin and seeds from 2 lb watermelon, cut into 1 inch cubes, and thread onto 8 metal skewers. Make the mint sugar as above, then sprinkle over the kebabs. Grill or broil the kebabs for 3–4 minutes on each side. Serve 2 kebabs per person.

Watermelon, Lime, and Mint Salad

Remove the skin and seeds from 2 lb watermelon, cut into cubes, and place in a large bowl. Drizzle with the juice of 2 limes and 2 teaspoons grated lime rind. Let steep for 20 minutes. Make the mint sugar as above and serve with the fruit salad.

DES-HEAL-FYY

Baked Red Fruit and Hazelnut Meringues

Serves 4

2 extra-large egg whites
½ cup superfine sugar
¼ cup ground toasted hazelnuts
2 cups hulled and halved
  strawberries
3 cups raspberries

- Beat the egg whites in a clean bowl with a handheld electric mixer until they form soft peaks, then gradually beat in the sugar until the mixture is thick and glossy. Gently fold in the hazelnuts.

- Mix together the strawberries and the raspberries in a bowl and divide among four 1 cup ramekins or ovenproof dishes. Pile the meringue on top of each.

- Place on a baking sheet and bake in a preheated oven, at 400°F, for 7 minutes or until the meringues are browned. Serve immediately.

Red Fruit Meringue Creams

Break up 2 meringue nests and place in the bottom of 4 glasses. Place 1 cup raspberries and ¾ cup hulled and sliced strawberries in a bowl and sprinkle over 1 tablespoon superfine sugar. Crush the fruit slightly with a fork, then spoon over the meringue. Mix together 1 cup reduced-fat crème fraîche, 1 cup fat-free Greek yogurt, and 1 tablespoon superfine sugar in a bowl, then stir in 2 crushed meringue nests. Spoon on top of the fruit and serve immediately.

Hazelnut and Raspberry

Meringue Roulade Beat 5 egg whites in a clean large bowl with a handheld electric mixer until stiff, then gradually beat in heaping 1 cup superfine sugar until the mixture is thick and glossy. Gently fold in ½ teaspoon white wine vinegar, ½ cup ground toasted hazelnuts, and 1 teaspoon cornstarch. Spread the mixture into an 8 x 12 inch jelly roll pan lined with nonstick parchment paper. Place in the center of a preheated oven, at 350°F, for 15 minutes. Let cool in the pan for 5 minutes. Turn out the meringue onto another piece of parchment paper. Mix together 1 cup Greek yogurt, 1 cup low-fat crème fraîche, and 2 tablespoons superfine sugar in a bowl. Spread evenly over the meringue and sprinkle with 1 cup raspberries. Roll up the meringue and serve immediately.

Pineapple and Mint Salad

Serves 4

1 ripe pineapple
3 tablespoons chopped mint
grated rind and juice of 1 lime
1 red chili, seeded and finely
   chopped (optional)

- Cut the top and bottom off the pineapple. Hold the pineapple firmly, resting it on the cut bottom. Slice off the skin, working from top to bottom, removing any brown "eyes." Cut into quarters lengthwise, remove the tough core in the center, and cut into cubes.

- Place in a large bowl and stir in the mint, lime rind and juice, and chili, if using. Stir well to combine and serve immediately.

2. Pineapple and Mint Salsa

Slice the skin from 1 pineapple as above, then cut into ½ inch thick circles and remove the tough core in the center using an apple corer. Place a ridged grill pan or nonstick skillet over medium heat, add the pineapple in a single layer, and cook for 3–4 minutes on each side until charred. Remove from the skillet and repeat with remaining pineapple. Chop the pineapple into small chunks, place in a bowl, and squeeze over the juice of 2 limes. Add 2 tablespoons chopped mint and mix well. Serve immediately.

3. Grilled Pineapple Kebabs with Chili and Mint Syrup

Prepare the pineapple as above and cut into cubes. Thread onto 8 metal skewers and place in a shallow dish. To make the chili syrup, place 1 medium red chili, seeded and thinly sliced, the grated rind and juice of 1 lime, ⅔ cup superfine sugar, and ⅔ cup cold water in a saucepan and stir over low heat until the sugar has dissolved. Bring to a boil, then reduce the heat and simmer for 10 minutes until syrupy. Let cool slightly, then stir in 3 tablespoons chopped mint. Pour over the pineapple and let stand for about 5 minutes. Preheat a ridged grill pan until hot, add the kebabs, and cook for 8 minutes, turning occasionally. Serve 2 kebabs per person with any remaining syrup.

 Instant Raspberry Sorbet

Serves 4

2½ cups frozen raspberries

2 tablespoons superfine sugar

2 tablespoons water

1 tablespoon crème de framboise
(raspberry liqueur) (optional)

fresh raspberries, to serve

- Place the raspberries, sugar, measured water, and crème de framboise, if using, in a food processor. Blend for 2–3 minutes until all the ingredients are blended and start to come together.

- Serve scoops of sorbet immediately in bowls with fresh raspberries or place in a freezerproof container and freeze until ready to use.

2 **Raspberry Sorbet Meringues**

Make the raspberry sorbet as above. Spread 1 tablespoon of the sorbet on each side of 2 meringue shells, then sandwich them together. Place in the freezer. Repeat with 6 more meringue shells. Remove from the freezer and serve immediately, drizzled with a little store-bought fruit coulis.

3 **Raspberry Sorbet Chocolate-Dipped**

Cones Melt 2 oz semisweet dark chocolate, broken into small pieces, in a heatproof bowl set over a saucepan of gently simmering water. Remove from the heat and dip the ends of 4 waffle cones into the melted chocolate, then roll the ends in ½ cup chopped pistachios. Stand in glasses and chill until set. Make the raspberry sorbet as above and serve in scoops in the cones.

 # Tropical Fruit Salad with Ginger Green Tea Syrup

Serves 6

2 large mangoes, peeled,
pitted, and cut into
1 inch chunks

2 large papaya, peeled, seeds
removed, and cut into chunks

1 small pineapple, skinned, cored,
and cut into 1 inch chunks (see
page 242)

2 kiwifruit, peeled and cut
into chunks

2¾ cups drained canned lychees

1⅔ cups green grapes

For the syrup

⅔ cup superfine sugar

1¼ cups water

grated rind and juice of 1 lime

1 inch piece of fresh ginger root,
peeled and chopped

1 green tea teabag

- To make the syrup, place the sugar, measured water, lime rind and juice, and ginger in a saucepan and heat gently, stirring occasionally, until the sugar has dissolved. Bring to a boil and simmer for 5 minutes.

- Remove from the heat and add the teabag, then let steep for 10 minutes. Remove the teabag and pour into a pitcher. Chill for 10 minutes to let the syrup steep and cool.

- Place all the prepared fruit in a large bowl and strain over the cooled syrup. Serve immediately or chill until ready to serve.

---

1 Tropical Fruit Kebabs

Prepare 2 mangoes, 1 papaya, and 1 pineapple as above and cut into cubes. Thread the prepared fruit with 2¾ cups of drained canned lychees, alternately, onto 12 metal skewers. Place on a baking sheet and sprinkle with the grated rind and juice of 2 limes and 2 tablespoons light brown sugar. Cook under a preheated hot broiler for 3–4 minutes or until the sugar starts to caramelize.

2 Tropical Fruits with Passion Fruit

Syrup Place ⅓ cup water and 2 tablespoons superfine sugar in a small saucepan and stir over low heat until the sugar has dissolved, then add a 1 inch piece of peeled and sliced fresh ginger root. Simmer for 3 minutes, then let cool for 10 minutes. Meanwhile, prepare 2 mangoes, 2 papaya, and 1 small pineapple as above and cut into thin circles. Place the syrup in a blender and add the pulp and

seeds of 4 passion fruit, then process for 10 seconds. Pour the syrup over the fruits and serve immediately.

Gooseberry and Elderflower Fools

Serves 4

3 cups gooseberries
  or diced kiwifruit
¼ cup elderflower syrup
¼ cup superfine sugar
1¾ cups reduced-fat
  crème fraîche

- Place the gooseberries, syrup, and sugar in a saucepan and bring to a boil, then partly cover with a lid. Simmer for about 8 minutes or until soft.

- Transfer to a food processor or blender and process until smooth. Pour into a large bowl and chill for 5 minutes until cool.

- Place the crème fraîche in a bowl and stir in two-thirds of the gooseberry puree. Spoon the fool into 4 glasses and top with the remaining puree. Serve immediately or chill until ready to serve.

10 Gooseberry and Elderflower

Compote Place 3 cups gooseberries or diced kiwifruit, ¼ cup elderflower syrup, and 3 tablespoons sugar in a saucepan and simmer, uncovered, for 8–10 minutes, stirring occasionally. Add a little more sugar to taste if necessary. Serve with dollops of Greek yogurt

30 Gooseberry and Elderflower Crisp

Place 4½ cups gooseberries or chopped rhubarb in a 1 quart ovenproof dish. Sprinkle over ⅓ cup superfine sugar and 2 tablespoons elderflower syrup. Place 1 cup whole-wheat flour and ⅓ cup low-fat spread in a bowl and rub together with the fingertips until the mixture resembles fine bread crumbs. Alternatively, use a food processor. Stir in 1 cup muesli and 2 tablespoons superfine sugar. Sprinkle the topping over the fruit and press down lightly. Place in a preheated oven, at 350°F, for 20–25 minutes until golden and bubbling.

DES-HEAL-BYV

Index

Acknowledgments

Executive editor: **Eleanor Maxfield**
Senior editor: **Leanne Bryan**
Copy-editor: **Jo Murray**
Art director: **Jonathan Christie**
Design: **www.gradedesign.com**
Art direction: **Juliette Norsworthy & Tracy Killick**
Photographer: **Will Heap**
Home economist: **Denise Smart**
Stylist: **Isabel De Cordova**
Senior production controller: **Lucy Carter**